THE ONLY NEGOTIATION BOOK YOU'LL EVER NEED

Winning Maneuvers for the DIGITAL AGE!

THE ONLY NEGOTIATION BOOK YOU'LL EVER NEED

Winning Maneuvers for the DIGITAL AGE!

>>
- Find the negotiation style that's right for you
- Avoid common pitfalls
- Maintain composure during high-pressure negotiations
- Negotiate any deal—without giving in

ANGELIQUE PINET AND PETER SANDER

Avon, Massachusetts

Published by
Adams Media, a division of F+W Media, Inc.
57 Littlefield Street, Avon, MA 02322. U.S.A.
www.adamsmedia.com

Previously published in electronic form under the title *Split-Second Negotiation*
by Angelique Pinet and Peter Sander, copyright © 2011 by F+W Media Inc.,
ePub ISBN 10: 1-4405-2918-3, ePub ISBN 13: 978-1-4405-2918-4.

ISBN 10: 1-4405-6072-2
ISBN 13: 978-1-4405-6072-9
eISBN 10: 1-4405-6073-0
eISBN 13: 978-1-4405-6073-6

Printed in the United States of America.

10   9   8   7   6   5   4   3   2   1

This publication is designed to provide accurate and authoritative information
with regard to the subject matter covered. It is sold with the understanding that
the publisher is not engaged in rendering legal, accounting, or other professional advice. If legal advice or other expert assistance is required, the services
of a competent professional person should be sought.

—From a *Declaration of Principles* jointly adopted by a Committee of the
American Bar Association and a Committee of Publishers and Associations

Many of the designations used by manufacturers and sellers to distinguish
their product are claimed as trademarks. Where those designations appear in
this book and Adams Media was aware of a trademark claim, the designations
have been printed with initial capital letters.

This book is available at quantity discounts for bulk purchases.
For information, please call 1-800-289-0963.

Contents

Chapter 3
Prepare the Ground / 35

Chapter 4
Find Your Negotiating Style / 55

Chapter 10
Under Contract / 159

Chapter 11
Negotiating for the Long Term / 175

Introduction

THE DIGITAL AGE HAS changed everything—including negotiation.

Ten years ago, negotiations might take place in a conference room, with the parties facing off against one another backed by PowerPoint slides containing myriad bullet points, charts, graphs, and statistics. Weeks or months might have gone into preparation for these sessions. Today such negotiations are often completed in a matter of hours, not days and weeks. Sometimes, important deals can even be struck in minutes.

This is the result of the age in which we live—one in which communication occurs at the speed of thought, in which e-mails zip back and forth and virtually everyone is plugged in twenty-four hours of every day through cell phones, BlackBerries, iPads, and every other device you can imagine.

The basics of negotiating have not changed. All the old rules still apply: you must know your bargaining position, your walkaway point, and the other party's strengths and weaknesses. You must still understand what tactics and strategies work and which should be discarded. What has changed in today's negotiations is *speed*—the speed at which the exchanges take place and the vast increase in the amount and speed of resources that are available to the skilled negotiator.

This is the reason for this book, *The Only Negotiation Book You'll Ever Need*. Its aim is to ensure that in today's fast-paced world, you will not be left behind. We'll look at both negotiating tactics and the evolving tools of the digital age and see how the latter enhances the former.

Speed shouldn't frighten you. Rather, you should welcome it, since it means you can be more productive, more informed, and more effective. You'll plunge into the waters of negotiation and emerge triumphant. Why? Because you'll know how to gather information and make the best use of it to get what you want—when you need it.

Chapter 1
The Split-Second Imperative

IMAGINE THAT YOU ARE the CEO of ConWireless, a medium-sized electronics manufacturer. For some time you've been casting about for another, similar company to merge with in order to expand your retail operations. Now you've found someone: Electronics Shack, a company with a chain of stores throughout the country. It seems a perfect match. The Board of Directors has approved exploratory talks with the aim of a merger between the two companies, and upper management at Electronics Shack has responded favorably to your overtures. Your staff has done extensive research; you've stared at seemingly endless files and spreadsheets and mastered reams of facts and figures about Electronics Shack. You've discussed the matter in countless meetings with the board and your management team. It's all done. Now you're ready to go.

Though the preparation for this moment seemed endless, you know that as the talks begin everything's about to speed up—dramatically. You live in an age of split-second decision making, when every issue, every detail, every concern of each side will have to be addressed and resolved quickly. You'll have to discuss with your counterpart of Electronics Shack what would constitute a fair deal for the stockholders of the two companies. Who should be on the new board of directors? How should the responsibilities of manufacturing and retail be divided?- For that matter, who should be CEO—you or someone else?

On a more nitty-gritty level, you'll need to arrange new titles for executives, possibly new offices for corporate headquarters to accommodate a larger staff, and how and at what pace the merger, if it's concluded, will take place. You'll have to agree on the best way to announce it, both to the public and to your employees, many of whom may be concerned for their jobs in the new company.

No matter how many items you add to your To Do list, it always seems as if there are more. That's because complex projects such as this touch many people. In fact, in today's interconnected world, *anything* you do touches many people. Those potentially affected can include everyone from top management to a range of employees throughout the organization, including the IT department, manufacturing, the finance department, human resources, warehouse employees, and others. The project may also affect those outside the organization—in this case, your customers and various suppliers, all of whom will have to adjust to working with the larger merged company.

All these parties, actions, costs, terms and conditions, and deadlines will require agreements. And those agreements will have to be made quickly to match the pace of the rest of the corporate world—especially your competitors, who'll be watching you eagerly, looking for any signs of weakness on your part. These agreements in turn require negotiations—negotiations to come to terms with people throughout the organization so that they can work together in a new structure with a minimum of disruption. Successful negotiations with all these parties will ultimately depend on you; no one else will do it for you. You'll have to get management on board with each of the final decisions you negotiate, up to and including the final due date for the completion of each stage of the merger.

Danger—Fast Track Ahead

This is the reality of today's fast-paced world. Negotiation is a basic part of life, and it happens all around us. Although some might think that negotiating about a project takes away time from managing it, in point of fact negotiating is—*is*—part of managing the project. It's a big part, and a bigger part than ever in most projects encountered and tackled in today's commercial world. Why? We'll discuss that later.

All this negotiating *has to be done faster than ever before.* These days, business, technology, and products—and mergers—all move at a blinding speed. So does your competition, and if you don't keep up with them, you'll be left behind. In the case of the merger mentioned above, for instance, you might typically get three to six months to complete the integration of the two companies. Within that time, the entire commercial landscape around you can change.

The result, as indicated in the introduction, is that negotiations occur very quickly. Often they are tucked into odd moments of the day as executives and employees tap relentlessly on their BlackBerries.

These days there is no longer time to hold face-to-face meetings with the players involved. Some part of the negotiations—maybe the whole thing—will be done by e-mail, phone, IM, and even text.

The goal is to get what you need, get what you want, as quickly as possible so you and your organization can move forward without delays. But even at this accelerated pace, you must beware of harmful concessions or oversights. That's your goal.

The tactics you employ come from an assortment of traditional negotiating techniques, all sped up to accomplish the win-win. But even when the negotiation has been concluded and the terms agreed upon, you're not done—when running fast, in split-second mode, it's important to come away with what you want, as well as to preserve a long-term relationship with the other party. Why? Because you'll be working with these people in the future.

The changes in the speed of business are a reflection of structural changes in the nature of business and commerce itself. Whereas ten or twenty years ago it might take a long time—several years, possibly—for a product to go from prototype to finished commodity, today businesses move far more quickly. They try to respond to a rapidly changing customer base, one that's plugged into the Internet and gets its information at the speed of light. All of the technology that developed in the 1980s and 1990s—personal computers, voicemail, e-mail, cell phones—has crested in a never-ending wave of innovation.

This creates a snowball effect—fast here requires fast there, and pretty soon, everybody is trying to eke out the slightest competitive advantage before the competition gets there. "Publish or perish" is a long-standing epigram inside academia—and it applies to industry as well. Companies must produce competitive products more swiftly. To maintain their place in the industry, they must go faster, and to go faster, they must *negotiate* faster. It's a model duplicated everywhere.

So what does that mean for you? Simply, you must go faster too. You must become more productive; you must learn to use the tools, do many things at once, and do them well. You can't hold up the process. Delays don't just add to the cost of a product, they detract from its market life. And if you can't be a fast enough cog in this new machine, you'll be quickly discarded and replaced.

Technology Gamechangers

With the exception of organizing data and creating nice presentation slides, personal computers, at least initially, didn't do much to change the world of negotiation. This was in part because the devices weren't widespread.

Second, few people had the accompanying products and materials to really make them work—the software and data in the case of the PC, the network coverage and unlimited minute plans of the cell phone, or the facility and ease of use of the Internet browser.

Over the course of a few years these new techno-fads became business reality. Initially, they were a novelty. They barely worked, and they didn't work with each other as an integrated platform. Businesses, and business*people*, had to learn how to *use* them.

▶ Real-Time Data Acquisition

Today electronic and communications devices enable real-time data acquisition, data management, and communication tools. Since all of these things are key parts of a negotiation, it's not hard to see how negotiating has changed forever.

Three things have changed, actually:

1. *Ubiquitous use.* Almost everyone on this planet—at least in the "rich" world—has learned to use the big-game changers—the Internet, mobile phones, e-mail—to their advantage. More importantly, if you *don't* use these devices, you're out of the loop.

2. *Shorter learning curves.* It takes less time for these devices to take hold. People have an appetite and a mindset for new devices and can figure out how to deploy them for "fast" business results more quickly. And the corollary products are there, too. Witness the Apple iPad and tablet computing, and its "apps," and how that's changing portable web browsing and computing. Ultimately and rather quickly, the advent of tablets will impact negotiating.

3. *Integration.* Instead of lugging around three mobile devices— a laptop, a PDA, and a pager—and still having to find a hotel room with a cable to log into the office, you can use today's devices to connect with each other from anywhere. You can send a mobile text to someone's e-mail. You can use the mobile to access a web page or critical piece of corporate data—right now.

▶ Facing Facebook

Beyond these hardware devices, people are connected in ways never dreamed of just ten years ago. Facebook, LinkedIn, and simple references obtained through Google or some other search engine search can inform us about and connect us to people in ways never thought of before. Not only do you have the hardware to communicate with "the network" but you also have platforms to get in touch, stay in touch, and find out more.

As much as anything else, Facebook has trained us to stay in touch in real time, all the time. And that has obvious implications for a negotiation. Many negotiations continue in real time through virtual networks and venues until they are done—not in the conventional day-long face-to-face conference room negotiating session of days past.

Of course, what it all means is that any negotiation can happen anywhere, using any device. You must either become part of this picture—or be left behind.

Do It Yourself

Thirty or forty years ago most of us in any kind of medium- or large-sized business had help to navigate the choppy waters of business. There was a support staff and support team. Secretaries, administrative assistants, sales development people, contracts people, even professional negotiators were in the office or nearby to help us research and develop business deals. We determined what needed to be done, what needed to be researched, what needed to be written, and where the meeting was to be held. Someone else did the legwork.

The support staff set up the meeting, did the research, wrote memos, drew up proposals, took phone calls, and made sure everyone was ready to attend the meeting.

Now, of course—that's all changed. The PC and its software, e-mail, cell phones, and voicemail have made us all our own secretaries. The Internet has made us our own researchers and meeting arrangers. The connected network has made us into our own negotiators. Companies have cut their support staff to the bone, because so many of these functions have devolved onto the rest of us.

Corporate hierarchies, while they still exist, are easily transcended by electronic communication. What does that mean? It means that in most circumstances you've become your own negotiator.

There still are professional negotiators, and if you're one of these, you've probably already developed most of the skill sets outlined in this book. You are probably a *negotiating professional*. As such you need to incorporate negotiating skills into your broader set of tricks. You need to negotiate deals, deadlines, and dollars yourself to make the rest of your project—the rest of your *job*—move forward.

What's a Professional Negotiator?

What is the difference between a negotiating professional and a professional negotiator? A negotiating professional is probably someone who does something for a living, and has to negotiate once in a while to get it done. A professional negotiator negotiates for a living. She or he is a hired gun who goes forth to handle complex negotiations for others as a service. Most of us would fall into the category of negotiating professionals employing negotiating skills as one of many professional skills required to do our jobs.

Negotiating Is All Around Us

Not only must we do our own negotiating, but negotiating has become a constant way of life for most of us. We negotiate for our projects. We negotiate for new jobs, new projects, raises, flexible work schedules, and travel arrangements. We negotiate with internal individuals and organizations, and individuals and organizations on the outside. Rare is a day when you aren't in some kind of negotiation, either with an employee or direct supervisor or with someone external to your company.

Some of the bargaining we do is with people we seldom or never had to negotiate with before. We have to negotiate with our children. We have to negotiate with our schools. We have to negotiate with various players in our personal financial lives, including other members of a family. Negotiation has replaced a hierarchical order that was once much more present in families and in our personal lives.

Of course, not only is there more to negotiate over, but it's all going faster. Your teenagers will negotiate with you (though it may not seem like a negotiation) over their cell phone. They'll send you a link minutes beforehand showing you the car they want to buy, and God help you if you don't look at it before you talk. You negotiate who's picking you up when.

You're busy, so you've contracted a lot of home services, like mowing the lawn, to someone else. There's another negotiation. Is your mother coming for a visit today or tomorrow? There's another negotiation. You'd better check the weather first. Prepare (if you can), respond, and respond now.

Not only is there more to negotiate over, and not only does it all go faster, but everything changes faster too. New information arrives faster. The shipment will be late? Renegotiate the project due date, and renegotiate people's time and availability. Price change? Gotta deal with that. Kid just got invited to a friend's house (via a text message?). Negotiate that deal (probably also by text.)

The bottom line: if you're like most people, you spend most of your time these days working out some kind of arrangement with someone. It's a connected world. And because those connections are electronic, they operate in real time. To cope in this world, you need to execute split-second negotiating, and you need to execute it well.

With all that in mind, let's turn to the problem of negotiating in a vastly speeded-up world. To put this in the proper context, we need to go back to the basics of negotiation.

Split-Second Takeaways

1. Because of the speedy pace of technological change today, negotiators must increase the speed of their bargaining.

2. Split-second timing pervades all aspects of business, including production, management, finance, and other key players in negotiations.

3. You are probably not a professional negotiator, but you almost certainly are and will be a negotiating professional.

4. Negotiation is a basic part of our lives, and we have to learn to do it well and do it fast.

Chapter 2
Why Negotiate?

PERHAPS YOU HAVEN'T REALIZED it, but you've been playing the negotiating game all your life. You were doing it even before you entered the "real world" of business-to-business negotiations. It was part of your reality before negotiating "business-to-consumer" to buy a car or digital TV or satellite TV service. In today's world, you negotiate "consumer-to-consumer" for things you buy or sell on Craigslist and eBay.

This may seem far away from the kind of negotiating you did when you were a child, trading baseball cards or swapping lunches at school. However, tapping into the core skills you developed during all those scrimmages is easy once you learn where your innate desire to "swap" originated.

While those days may have long faded into history, the practice and promise of negotiating has most likely stayed with you—and most likely has become more important than ever in the "real life" you lead today.

Bartering Back Through Time

So where, how, when, and why did negotiation become a part of civilized society? It really started as barter—the direct exchange of goods or services without money involved.

No one really knows when the first barter took place, but we do know that bartering has been around for much longer than buying and selling. It grew up as a system of give-and-take that accommodated anyone who chose to participate. Whether it was to acquire a piece of lamb in exchange for some pottery or to obtain jewelry for a hand-painted headpiece, people found ways to fulfill their needs.

Negotiate Now!

Bartering at the Speed of Light

Bartering is an exchange of goods or services without the use of money as an item of value or to equalize the transaction. The worth of the objects or services being exchanged is up to the two parties involved, and negotiation is how the two parties establish exact worth. In today's world, such an exchange can take place almost instantly, negotiated through e-mail between the two participants. Because of the vastly greater information available to both of you through the Internet, you can more quickly equate the worth of different goods or services, agree on a common exchange rate, and set the terms of the barter.

Bartering was a way to acquire life's necessities, but it was more than that—it broke down the barriers of communication. When people met for the first time, bartering was a way to observe if the person was trustworthy and genuine, and only after mutual willingness to trade was expressed would a dialogue between the two parties ensue. (This is equally true today in many cultures, particularly when so much of our interaction occurs in cyberspace.)

Bartering didn't have to be immediate—the exchange could take place at two different points of time. For example, when guests visited someone's home, they brought along gifts as a sign of respect and gratitude. Later, when the guests departed, the host would give them something of his own to take with them for the journey home.

Eventually, bartering slowly evolved into a primitive financial arrangement, in which cows, sheep, and other livestock were used as the first forms of currency. Plants, produce, and other agricultural items also served as currency, only to be overtaken by precious metals, stones, and finally paper bills.

The First Money

Cowries—marine snails boasting thick, glossy shells peppered with tiny flecks—appeared in China in 1200 B.C. as the first objects to be used as money. They were widely used, and even became popular in faraway places like Africa, where some cultures continue to exchange them today. Cowries are the longest-used currency in history. In this modern era of real-time foreign exchange quotes, we still have no idea how many cowries there are to a dollar. However, as should be obvious from a swift scan of the financial news, enormous sums of money flow instantly through the ether as groups of 0s and 1s as banks and other institutions transfer money by electronic means.

From Bargaining to Negotiating

When people bartered, most of the time they knew the values of the objects they exchanged. Suppose that three baskets of corn were generally worth one chicken. Two parties had to persuade each other to execute the exchange, but they didn't have to worry about setting the price. But what if one year there was a drought and there wasn't much corn to go around? Then a farmer with three baskets of corn could perhaps bargain to exchange them for two or even three chickens. Bargaining the exchange value of something is a form of negotiating. And it works once you switch to a currency system.

As "primitive" as this sounds, most likely you've seen it in person. The way people bargain with each other varies from culture to culture, but you've seen it before at your local yard sale or flea market. The vendor gives you a price, you give the vendor a price, and eventually either a happy medium is decided upon or you walk away. More often than not, the vendor inches down on her price while you inch up on your price, until you're both at a number that doesn't allow either one of you to budge any more!

A different type of bargaining can be seen at an auction, where a roomful of people view the items up for sale and make their bids on the items they wish to buy. If someone outbids them, they're then given the opportunity to up their bid. This continues back and forth until one person has outbid all interested parties. Today, millions of people search for, post, trade, barter, bid, and buy anything from toys they had as children to signed sports paraphernalia on eBay and other Internet auction sites. If only our sheep-trading ancestors could see us now!

The Difference Between Bargaining and Negotiating

While the terms "bargaining" and "negotiating" seem synonymous, there's a distinct difference between the two. *Bargaining* involves streamlining wants and needs into a single focus. Before you ever step foot on the lawn where your neighbor's yard sale is taking place, you know in your mind that all the hand-written sticker prices are not permanent. Your goal is to get the item you desire at the lowest price possible. Your neighbor's goal on the other hand, is twofold— she wants to get rid of as many items as possible, and she wants to get the most amount of money for them.

Always Ask the Price

Whenever you're shopping—whether at a yard sale or online at Craigslist or a similar site, always establish what the price of the item is. If the seller responds with a question of her own—how much do you want to pay for it?—don't give up. Instead, insist on getting a price quote. Of course, when you're on the selling end, get the customer to give you a price. If it's too low you can turn it down, but if it's higher than what you had in mind, congratulate yourself!

When it comes to bargaining, everyone's focus is limited and all efforts are spent trying to get the best deal—for themselves. In this case, money is the focal point, and that's when the price war begins: "How much?" "A dollar." "I'll give you fifty cents." "Eighty cents." "Sixty cents." "Seventy cents." "Sixty-five cents." "Deal."

When a goal becomes concentrated, it's easy to lose sight of all the things that are really important. In the yard-sale example, price takes precedence over the usefulness of the product. The purchaser never stops to think, "If I thought it was worth only fifty cents a minute ago, why do I think it's worth more now?" Although the settled price was split equally down the middle, one person spent more than they intended to and the other person received less money for the item than they hoped to receive. So who got the bargain?

Some people are said to "drive a hard bargain," meaning there's little to no chance of swaying them away from believing their offer is fair. You can't bargain with them—they are convinced that they know best or that there's someone out there who'll pay the full price. Thus, the department-store mentality is born, and the only way you're ever paying a lower price is if there's a sale.

Negotiating, on the other hand, more generally refers to the art and science of agreeing on something or settling a question between two parties. The question may be about a barter transaction, or more simply about price, but it usually involves more than that. It takes in all attributes of a deal. Delivery, timing, extras, the right to negotiate a future deal—you name it. Really, more often than not people who negotiate are making an agreement on how to behave toward each other.

The Negotiating Game

A good negotiation draws on the skills used for marketplace bartering and on the focused determination required of bargaining. Negotiating encompasses a wide range of core principles and becomes a series of tactics and strategies that you must know how and when to use throughout the entire game. In addition to remaining focused and forging strong relationships, you'll need to be informed, be prepared, know who your challengers are, and have other alternatives.

And in today's fast-paced world, the game can be very short, and it can be done with a few tweets or IMs. But keep in mind—it is still a game, and it still has all the rules of a longer, more protracted exercise. It just happens faster.

Types of Negotiation

Although several forms of negotiation will be discussed in this book, the two most common are *positional* negotiating and *win-win* negotiating. Particularly in today's fast-paced and heavily interconnected world, you should be aware of both types of negotiation and should embrace win-win negotiation as the more favorable approach.

▶ ### Positional Negotiation

Positional negotiating occurs when neither side moves from its original position because both are so focused on their own needs that they cannot even begin to comprehend those of the other party. A power struggle ensues and they never really discuss goals and objects. The result is hours of trying to produce agreements that everyone is satisfied with; long-term relationships are jeopardized because there's too much negativity being exhibited. Time is wasted, because in today's environment an hour is forever. In positional negotiating, everyone is out for himself, and that's that.

As you might surmise, positional negotiations are very "one way" and typically don't work. They can take—and waste—a lot of time, not to mention energy and personal capital. Today's "split-second" negotiating requires a different approach, not only due to time constraints but also to preserve your position in the social and business network; if you gain a reputation for one-sidedness and "tough guy" behavior, it is easy enough for your counterparts to find someone else. (Far easier than in the past, in fact, because in this electronic age their potential range of suppliers is much larger.)

▶ ### Win-Win Negotiation

So, the only way to avoid falling into the positional negotiating trap is to adopt a win-win strategy. "Win-win" means that *both* parties come away with their needs met. As such, mutual agreements can be made more easily.

To be successful at win-win negotiating, it's important to figure out what everyone else's needs are and make one's own needs flexible so everyone is willing to play fair. Decisions are reached more quickly, great strides are made toward building positive relationships, and everybody is happy when it comes time to walk out of the room.

Win-win negotiating is successful because everyone goes into it with a positive attitude, a firm understanding of how the game is played, and a professional approach to the situation at hand. With such an approach, there is trust, and where there is trust, there are more and better results *more quickly*. Simply put: if you want to do a successful split-second negotiation, start with a win-win "end" in mind.

It shouldn't surprise you that much of the remainder of this book is about win-win negotiation. We will continually illustrate the steps that make it such a gratifying way to do business.

Start from the End

If you really want to do a split-second negotiation, start with a win-win "end" in mind.

The Reasons Why

There are endless reasons why negotiations can be beneficial, and most of them have their roots deeply planted in the soil of our bartering ancestor's back yard. Aside from the obvious reasons why negotiations are used in the business world (to increase profit, to form large corporations by merging small businesses, to build reputations), the successes you can achieve on a smaller scale in your personal life carry just as much weight as those achieved by companies through their representatives.

You practice the art of negotiation every day—at work and at the store; at a restaurant, with your utility companies, insurance company, family, friends, and coworkers. If you really want coleslaw with that hamburger instead of the French fries on the menu, it's time to negotiate. If your utility bills constantly come due two days before payday, you might call the utility company to request the date of payment be pushed back. If the bakery at your grocery store carries packages of eight dinner rolls when you only need six, you might ask the clerk to take two out of the bag and price them accordingly. In these situations you're asking the company you regularly do business with for a concession. What you offer in return is your continued business and a positive opinion about the company's devoted services.

What Is a Concession?

A concession is when you yield to another person by giving him a privilege that you don't usually give to other people. For example, during a business meeting, an executive asks for a 10 percent cut in production costs. The other executive agrees to this concession, but she asks for one of her own in return—that products be delivered a month earlier than usual. In today's split-second world, a concession can also be about negotiating time or the process itself. For example, you can pay a higher price or accept a slower delivery if they waive certain approval requirements to finish the negotiation more quickly.

In effect, if two or more people have goals they can help each other reach, they can enter into a negotiation. Carpooling allows drivers to conserve gas mileage, limit the amount of wear and tear on their vehicles, and save on the cost of gas. So a discussion or an offer to carpool is a negotiation. Babysitting usually requires a teenager to forfeit her Saturday night, but it also gives her spending money for next weekend. It becomes a negotiation—a negotiation of the "win-win" variety.

When They Don't Want to Play

Since negotiations require two or more, what do you do if the person you want to negotiate with refuses your offer? First, find out why. There may be a simple explanation. Maybe the person doesn't have the time to take you up on your offer just yet but would be willing to work with you at a later date.

If you can't find out why, find out what or how. What can you put forth in order to make your proposal more attractive? What can you put forth to make the negotiation quicker or easier? If the coworker you carpool with decides she likes the freedom of having her own car every day, remind her of the benefits that carpooling provides. You could even offer to let her take your car to lunch or to run errands. By switching the focus on how the deal gives her an advantage, and by giving her something in return for the freedom she'd be giving up, she's more likely to agree to the terms. And if you don't have time to work out the details, simply offer to drive the first week—you'll have plenty of time in the car to flesh out the deal.

If You Don't Think Negotiating Is Part of Your Life . . .

Put simply, everyone negotiates. Parents negotiate with teachers; husbands negotiate with wives; brothers negotiate with sisters; defense attorneys negotiate with prosecuting attorneys. Even children exercise a form of negotiating. It's funny how adults are still playing the game of "I'll trade you this for that," only in a more sophisticated and refined manner.

▶ Negotiating for Business

While you may play down these personal-life negotiations, if you're in any kind of business or professional environment, you're probably negotiating a lot. Deals are done, budgets are created, money is spent or acquired through negotiation. Bridges are built, roads are repaired, high-rises are erected, public transportation is rerouted, and streets are named—and all the while, there's a group of professionals negotiating the details of these projects by presenting their ideas and strategies to the appropriate approving manager, approval committee, or board of directors. You may find yourself vying for a multimillion-dollar deal for your business—or for a $150 admission ticket to a trade show you'd like to attend. Both are negotiations, and both require much the same set of skills.

▶ Getting What You Want

In sum, negotiating is about getting what you want. Win-win negotiating is about getting what you want through the recognition of your goals, their goals, and finding a peaceful solution that sends everyone away with maximum satisfaction with minimal time consumed. In today's split-second world, time is not only of the essence, but also, with additional real-time information available at our fingertips helps us find that win-win more quickly and precisely than ever before.

Split-Second Takeaways

1. Negotiation is a part of life; it's all around us every day.

2. Negotiation is the art of two parties agreeing on something.

3. There are two kinds of negotiation: positional and win-win. Win-win is always preferable.

Chapter 3
Prepare the Ground

WE'VE DESCRIBED NEGOTIATION AS a game. There are rules, and beyond the rules, there are strategies and tactics to achieve your goal. Like a game, it is important to win; that is the goal and why you enter the negotiation in the first place. But unlike most games, as suggested in the previous chapter we like to see the opponent win, too. Why? Not so much because it's a goal, but because it's a *strategy*. Letting the opponent win also is a strategy to help us get what we want, and a strategy to help us get through the negotiation more quickly. As I've indicated, this is the essential difference between positional negotiation and win-win negotiation—and it's why the latter is preferable.

While negotiating may differ from game playing in some respects, it is more important to keep the similarities in perspective. Games are all about the players, and like any good player, it's important to have an all-inclusive understanding of your game or sport in order to keep your awareness sharp and your advantage strong. Preparation is essential to playing the game in the best and most efficient manner possible, and information is the lifeblood supporting preparation.

Know Yourself and Your Goals

Before doing any research into the facts, figures, and dynamics of a negotiation, it's important to figure out what you want out of the negotiation. If you're negotiating for the bridge contract, you may have a dollar figure in mind, with associated construction times, crew deployments, and other details to go with it. If you're negotiating with your fifteen-year-old, you may really want to stay home beside your cozy fire, but you also want him to enjoy the evening. Sizing up these "musts" and "wants" all works towards setting goals, which in turn becomes a framework for the negotiation.

Organizing your thoughts will give you direction and purpose, and the true focus of your plan will come into view. You should never walk into a negotiation unsure of what you're doing there or not quite decided on what you hope to achieve. The other party, potentially a seasoned negotiator, will use this to his advantage by taking a dominant standpoint and making the purpose of the meeting all about his needs. Additionally, because you're unsure about what's important to you, you'll have nothing to arm yourself with when he hurls a deluge of desired concessions at you.

To determine exactly what your goals are, begin by asking yourself the following questions:

- What do I hope to achieve?
- Why are these achievements important to me?
- What is my main goal?
- What are my secondary goals?
- What are my "musts" and "wants"?
- What steps do I need to take to be successful?
- What can prevent me from being successful?
- What am I prepared to do to overcome the obstacles?

It's a good idea to list all the goals you hope to achieve, even if some are direct results of others. Next, **identify your main goal**. If it's a complex negotiation, it helps to inventory your goals and to write them down. If it's a split-second negotiation with your son or some other smaller business deal, it's still a good idea to list a few goals in your head. Regardless of the "split-second" nature of the negotiation, time spent here can get you closer to what you want and save a lot of agony later on.

Goals can shape your negotiating position and negotiating strategy. Bringing your goals to the forefront is only the first step in the preparation process. Prioritizing goals gives you a deeper understanding of what you need to accomplish during the negotiation.

Keep It Real

Set realistic goals. If a goal is too far out of reach, you may feel as if you failed if you don't accomplish it, when in reality the goal just wasn't really attainable. Put differently, a goal too far out of reach prevents the win-win, because your opponent simply can't come up with anything good enough for you without destroying his or her own position. It's also important to be as specific as possible with your goals so you can track your progress toward achieving them.

▶ Prioritizing Your Goals

Your main goal should be the driving force behind your negotiating position. If you want to buy a car because you need a way to get to work every morning, your main goal is to buy a reliable vehicle. Secondary goals will concern comfort, features, appearance, and price. The means to achieve those goals include the choice of brand, style, model, new versus used, and financing. Within this set of goals you'll be able to prioritize which is most important, check them against the means, and use the means to ask for concessions and/or to reprioritize or reshape the goals.

▶ "See" the Deal

If you envision how the meeting will unfold, you can better prepare for potential situations. If you let your imagination run wild, you can imagine a variety of scenarios and plan how to handle them if they take place. Sparking the creative side of your brain even before the preparation stage gives you the opportunity to get ready for the unexpected by developing a myriad of protective strategies. For instance, if you concoct a hypothetical situation in which your counterpart suddenly brings more team members into the negotiation, you can then put together a plan for countering that move.

Form a Mental Picture

Developing a mental picture of what will take place beforehand also gives you the opportunity to analyze the negotiation from all angles, so you can devise a list of questions and gather suitable information. You'll also want to highlight areas where you foresee potential conflicts and figure out ways to prevent them from happening as well as solutions for overcoming them if they do happen. It may help you to note these down in a file and write them out. Assemble as many facts and figures as possible to counter each scenario. Data is a weapon, and the more you can accumulate, the better prepared you will be.

▶ Prepare Possible Concessions

As you're defining goals, keep in mind that the ability to be flexible may serve to your advantage at some point during the negotiation. While you don't want to easily give up any of your goals, you do want to keep an open mind about how you can adjust them if it means a mutual agreement can be reached.

As mentioned earlier, concessions can be used as adjusters to the negotiation, small gives and takes to help arrive at the best win-win solution in the negotiation. They are like tiny "chits" to be rationed wisely. Throughout the course of every negotiation, both parties will ask for one concession in exchange for another. Each party wants to walk out of the room feeling satisfied with the concessions that were agreed upon. If you did your homework—researched, prepared, practiced, and weighed alternatives—you should have a good idea of what concessions you're comfortable making—and what concessions you're comfortable asking for.

Check Out the Competition

In today's information age, it is possible to research negotiating points and concessions very quickly and easily. Find out what the competition offers—both price and service—and how it compares to your own and your adversary's offerings. You should do this beforehand, and depending on the negotiating venue and conditions, you can even do this in real time if you have Internet access.

▶ Concession Strategies and Tactics

When you make concessions during negotiations, here are some guidelines to keep in mind:

- Know how to present concessions, from least to most important. Getting the easy ones out of the way first allows you to direct the bulk of your time and energy to more important ones.
- Exhibit the same amount of resistance for every concession so the other party can't tell which concessions have more value to you and which ones do not. You never want the other party to feel like you've gotten more out of her than she's gotten out of you. Otherwise, she's likely to ask for a lot more concessions.
- For every concession you make, ask for one in return. For example, "I'll give you a discount if you make a higher down payment."
- Provide reasons for your requested concessions so the other party can understand why you're asking for them. For example, "I'd like a discount on the sticker price to be able to afford the monthly payments." You'll earn the other party's respect if you prove you're not asking for something just to see if you can get it.

Some experts believe you should always make the first concession. That way you retain control over the ones that are important to you. But others feel that letting the other party make the first concession allows you to take the prize if they overbid. Eventually, you'll develop your own style of negotiating, but for now go with what feels most comfortable to you. Tactics like these (and many more) will be discussed later in this book.

► Know Your Limitations

Everyone has limits—and you should, too. Knowing your limits prior to the negotiation is part of the negotiating process. It helps you stay focused on what's important and allows you to determine whether the agreement is acceptable. The course of a negotiation often changes, and new concessions and limitations have to be established. When this happens, you'll need to determine if your old limitations still apply.

Don't Reveal Weaknesses

Don't let the other party know what your limitations are—at least not right away. Making them privy to this information up front might make you seem confrontational and uncompromising. If you absolutely, positively won't spend more than $10,000 on that car, you might not want to disclose that right off, for you might miss out on a really great $10,200 car or another concession the car salesperson might make. However, if the other party is coming dangerously close to your limits, feel free to warn him that you don't plan to compromise or go any further on those particular issues.

What kinds of limits should you set? Like goals, limits should be flexible but steadfast. Think of them as your bodyguards, ready to protect you instantly, should danger threaten. As soon as you start feeling uncomfortable and things aren't going your way, call attention to your bodyguards so the other party knows they're about to lose your business.

► Know Your Alternatives

In order to set limits, you should first examine your alternatives. If you could walk away from a negotiation and still have several opportunities waiting, you can be liberal with what limits you set. That's why I can't stress enough: **Be sure to have other alternatives before you enter into a negotiation.** It's also good to know what alternatives the other party has lined up since this will determine the importance he places on his concessions

In today's split-second world, facts will come forward in rapid-fire mode. Moreover, negotiating positions, including concessions and limits, will be tested and modified often in a matter of seconds. You'll have to keep up, and you'll have to make split-second decisions on your own, and know where to access information quickly (like the dealer cost of that sunroof option on a car). If you're not prepared, and not able to keep up, your opponent may get an advantage—or may walk away to deal with the next customer or supplier.

Know Your Opponent

Your underlying strategy should be largely based on your negotiating opponent. Study your opponent's playing style, and learn as much as possible about why she's investing her time in the negotiation. By reviewing the other party's training, accomplishments, education, and work history, for example, you can better predict what her actions will be and therefore be more prepared to address them.

Try to get the specifics of what the other party's goals are so you can weigh your leverage against theirs and adjust your game plan if you need to. It's also a good idea to use the first few minutes of the meeting to discuss some of the objectives you share and those that you do not.

▶ Who IS This Person?

One of the first steps is to learn as much as you can about the other party's background. What is this person's title? Role in the organization? Background? What kinds of deals does he or she negotiate? What is his or her negotiating style?

In today's split-second information age, it's possible to find out more about people more quickly than ever. Google, Facebook, LinkedIn, plus the varied and multitudinous ways to network on your own, give you access to a treasure trove of information about your opponent. You can get a lot about the character of an individual and an organization just by looking around on the web and by tapping the network. Be sure to visit the company's web page and study the public records of previous negotiations they've engaged in. For example:

- Have they been involved in recent mergers or acquisitions, and if so what were the terms?
- Have they recently switched any significant vendors?
- Have they offered new products on the market?
- Does any of your sales staff have experience with them? Is there a company "negotiating culture"?

The Value of Google (and Other Search Engines)

The Internet is a remarkable tool for finding out anything about anyone anywhere in the world. Googling someone or something provides a list of websites that often contain valuable information. You'll be amazed at the number of "hits" you get on people. A small number of hits can reveal something too—the individual simply doesn't have much of a public persona. Finally, watch out for "multiple name syndrome"—where two or more individuals have the same name—which can throw you quite a ways off track.

▶ **Day of the Show**

For various reasons, concrete information about an opponent may be difficult to put together in advance. It still helps to do some research on the "day of the show"—when the negotiation happens.

Simply asking the other party a few open-ended questions before negotiations begin can give you some idea of whom you're dealing with. Though you can't assume the answers you receive are 100 percent accurate, ask questions like:

- "How long have you been with the company?"
- "How long have you been in your current position?"

- "What were your previous responsibilities within the company?"
- "Whom do you report to?"
- "What do you hope to gain from this negotiation?"

The answers may you get you to common goals more quickly and may indicate, to some extent, the possibility of a hidden agenda. For example, if the other party has been with the company for only three months, then she may be eager to prove herself to her superiors and try to exhibit an aggressive attitude. On the other hand, if the person you're negotiating with has held her position with the company for over fifteen years, she's bound to have a few tricks up her sleeve.

▶ It's a Question of Authority

When you prepare to deal with your opponent, consider how much leeway he has to make concessions and compromise. Is this person really authorized to make decisions, or is he merely a proxy for his manager and unable to make decisions on his own?

Whether you're negotiating with one person or five people, directly ask the participants one by one if they are authorized to negotiate with you and to make and agree to concessions. If you're negotiating with only one person and the answer is no, you will have saved yourself hours of wasted time by asking this important question up front. As soon as the other party reveals he is not authorized to make any deals with you, start packing your briefcase and ask if it would be possible to meet with the person who is authorized to negotiate.

Background Information

Arriving at a negotiation meeting without any notes, research findings, or information of any kind is like a football team going to their game without a game plan. You'll want to know everything you can about your opponent—their products, prices, business dealings, value propositions, market comparisons, financial performance, management style, strategies, tactics, practices, and anything else pertinent to your situation, be it buying your first home, a used car, or paint for the exterior of your garage. Just as importantly, you can get information about how others, including customers, *feel* about this organization and its products. If that paint really works—or not—you can find out, or at least get an impression, in a matter of minutes. If you don't get the knowledge, you'll at least *know what questions to ask.*

The Importance of the Internet

In today's split-second negotiation era, such things as Internet access wherever you happen to be conducting the negotiation can be critically important. The Internet can be used to research information on the fly to aid the discussion or make offers and concessions; it may also be vital for accessing other individuals in your organization or elsewhere as backup resources. Similarly, for those with 3G or 4G wireless devices, such service can be important. Always make sure WI-FI or cell access is available according to your needs—or plan accordingly if these are not available. The worst surprise is no Internet when you were depending on it.

In the old days, you could burn hours in a local library looking at magazine articles, company research reports, *Standard & Poor's* and *Moody's* and *Thomas Guides* and other large, heavy bound materials. It was a monumental task, and you weren't likely to get the most timely information, nor the "scoop" and "buzz" and other information you'd really want to bring to the party.

Today, the Internet levels that playing field. You can get all sorts of formally published information for a company's website and myriads of business and financial websites. Better yet, you can get less structured but sometimes more "real" and real-time commentary from Wikipedia, blogs, and other corners of the web—a Google search is powerful here, too. Within minutes, you can know a lot about an organization, its products, and its personality—and what others have felt and experienced from it.

Know the Right Questions

When you're researching an individual or an organization to learn more about it, it's important to get whatever facts and experiences are available. But remember—it's not just about the information you get—it's also about knowing what questions to ask.

▶ Get Firsthand Experience

Nothing prepares you for a situation quite like the way hands-on experience does. Don't be afraid to get your hands dirty! If you know you want to buy a car in the near future, visit a few different dealerships and talk to a variety of salespersons. This will give you exposure to their world as well as an up-close look at the kinds of tactics they employ and what types of questions they'll ask you. Study the tones of their voices and what information they choose to share with you.

If your daughter has been hinting that she'd love a new stereo system for her sixteenth birthday, prepare yourself ahead of time by visiting brick-and-mortar stores to look at what's available. If you want to know what the hottest stereo system is (the one all your daughter's friends are buying), visit the same stores frequently and take note of which models are collecting dust as opposed to which models seem to be flying off the shelves every week. Chances are, if everyone else loves it, your daughter will too.

They're Watching You

If a salesman doesn't approach you as soon as you step onto the car lot, more times than not he still knows you're there. He's deliberately waiting to approach you because he wants to monitor the way you look at the product. If he notices you're looking at the tires first, for instance, he'll walk over to you and mention something about the extended warranty their tires carry.

Analyze Your Alternatives

Having one or several alternative courses of action is key to negotiating successfully; indeed it will give you an advantage. You need to know what other parties you can negotiate with for the same thing, just as you want to know all the stores that carry that flat screen TV you're looking for. Alternatives provide you with the confidence to reject offers and to walk away from the negotiation if you're not happy with the way it's going. This is where your power comes from, so use it when you need it the most.

For example, imagine that there's only one car dealership in your town, and you need to buy a car. Think about how disappointed and dejected you would feel if your negotiations with the car dealer did not go at all the way you had hoped. The dealer would be well aware that his business was your only option, and he would take full advantage of the situation by making you agree to almost all of his concessions without having to agree to any of yours. Similarly, if you were the car dealer, what if the only customer who wanted to purchase a particular car decided to walk out the door? You'd either have to come up with even more concessions to try to get her to come back, or you'd just have to cut your losses.

In their renowned book *Getting to Yes* (1991), Roger Fisher and William Ury urge you to develop your Best Alternative To a Negotiated Agreement (BATNA) and follow it through so you always have something to measure against. If you plan to negotiate a raise from your boss, try to get another job offer before the discussion begins. This is your BATNA—your bargaining chip.

Essential Alternatives

Your alternatives represent part of what you have in your "back pocket" going into and through a negotiation. The analysis of alternatives thus becomes a critical part of your preparation. In split-second negotiating, you may have to call on these alternatives very quickly while they are still available. If you use the alternatives as a negotiating tool with your primary opponent, you must be prepared with accurate facts pretty much in real time, or else your credibility will disappear quickly. So you need to fact-check the alternatives quickly and frequently—and be able to recheck them in split-second time—during your negotiation. Don't be afraid to call a brief time out if necessary.

▶ Plan B and Beyond

Whatever you're negotiating, you need to have at least one Plan B that's as lucrative as your original plan—or else you won't feel it's worth aspiring to when Plan A fails. Plan B should be carefully cultivated under the guise that it's actually an A-Plan. The same amount of research, prodding, and strategizing must be applied so you can spring right back into action if your original plan falls through. The more solid alternatives you have under your belt, the more poise you'll exhibit in front of the other party who—make no mistake about it—will probably sense the air of self-assurance that surrounds you.

▶ Using Alternatives to Your Advantage

Unquestionably, the other party will have his own set of alternatives to bring to the table. Discovering what other options your negotiating adversary has lined up allows you to assess the level of confidence he has and to determine how much leverage the both of you have. If he doesn't have any options, or the ones you perceive he does have are weak, then you have the upper hand. Now, you may be tempted to have a lot of fun with this and get every little concession you can out of him. However, be mindful that some day the tables may be turned, and you'll be the one with no or few alternatives.

The Meeting Itself

Business negotiating meetings used to all occur in a physical location like a conference room or meeting room, somewhere in an office or hotel, or some other defined venue. Today, business negotiations, and most personal negotiations, can happen almost anywhere—whether it's over e-mail or by phone. Most of the more important negotiations are planned, but many are spontaneous. With planned negotiations, there is an opportunity for some strategy and control of the meeting, including the place, time, and agenda.

Preparing an agenda for the meeting will help you stay focused, as well as help keep everyone else on track. The other party may also have a schedule to follow, in which case you'll have to compare both schedules to make sure everything gets covered. The agenda should allow for discovery, presentation of alternatives, and making the deal or other actions such as further research constructive to the deal.

The agenda sequence, presenters, topics, desired outcomes, time allotted for "free" time and even breaks and lunches are all important elements of the agenda. The agenda can be used to help steer the conversation towards the goals you want to achieve, by adjusting time allotments for factual presentations, discussions, and desired outcomes. By controlling the agenda you control the pace of the process, and the process can proceed "in synch" with your objectives— or not. It also helps to be the discussion moderator or leader—you can adjust the meeting content and format, often in real time, to achieve what you want to achieve.

Set a Schedule

In addition to keeping the meeting on track, schedules help remind everyone what has already been covered and what still needs to be addressed. There may be certain issues the other party hopes to avoid. Listing them on the schedule lets them know that those issues are important to you and that they will need to be discussed.

▶ Without an Agenda

Sometimes the best way to reinforce the need to do something is to describe what happens if you *don't* do it. The consequences of not setting an agenda or schedule are a good illustration.

Control the Agenda

Think there's no use for an agenda in a split-second negotiation? Think again. It helps to lay out a quick-and-dirty agenda even for a simple phone call or e-mail discussion. This gets the other party to agree on what the objective is, how much time will be spent on each topic, and what the desired outcome is—even if the negotiation is just for a few minutes. It helps to keep things on track and avoid leaving important items out. It also gives you some control over the meeting and hence, the negotiation. Always think in terms of setting—and controlling—the agenda.

A meeting agenda works as your backup and outline for your meeting, helping you to achieve all of your objectives in the shortest time possible. Without a schedule in hand, your meeting can turn into chaos. Everyone will be thinking about a different issue, and no one will know when to transition from one to another. The velocity of the meeting may be too fast, causing some subjects to be overlooked and other subjects to be discussed too quickly. Allowing ample time for every subject is vital in making steps toward progress. Reserve large chunks of time for heartier matters that will be examined more carefully and in more detail. Trivial matters that need to be dealt with shouldn't use up a lot of your valuable time—they can be handled simply and efficiently.

Case Study:
Getting the Negotiating Picture

You're the president, CEO, and CPO (Chief Photography Officer) of RGB Photographic, a small firm (really, just you most of the time) engaged in commercial photography mainly in your local market. You have some helpers and associates you contract with on an as-needed basis, and your brother-in-law, a stay-at-home dad, helps you from time to time with administrative work and with delivering the pictures. You have a range of other suppliers and services, including photofinishers and a helicopter service at your disposal for aerial photos, among others.

You are trying to secure a deal with a big client: Trindle and Trundle Associates, a big nationwide developer with an office and commercial real estate development operations in your market, Shady City, California. You want to get a juicy regular gig shooting new developments every month so that the local boys can give the big corporate boys, their clients, and their investors a full progress update. If you get an "exclusive" for this job, it would mean an extra $15 to $20,000 in monthly revenues, which would go a long way towards making your year.

But you must negotiate successfully.

So, as we've learned in this chapter, that means among other things:

1. Setting good goals

2. Knowing your client

3. Evaluating alternatives and concessions to secure at least part of the business for yourself

4. Being prepared for the day of the negotiation

Below is a brief summary of the thought process you might go through. If you were doing this for real, these might be more completely thought out and documented, something you might do yourself or with a partner or sounding board over a nice dinner or refreshments.

Goal setting

Main goal: Get all the business; become Trindle's exclusive Shady City photographer.

Secondary goals: Get a substantial portion of the business, say, the aerial photos, or shooting the images while they rely on their own in-house marketing team to produce the images. Another goal, of course, is to build a relationship so they will call you with one-time or ad-hoc, irregular pieces of business when their main source gets busy.

Concessions and alternatives

Photographers have myriads of concessions at their disposal. They can offer free prints, they can do the computerized photofinishing and layout, they can give rights to the images or not, they can arrange for a full service, including aircraft rental, or not. Delivery time is another important factor. You need to be ready to put together some kind of package deal.

As the chief negotiator, run through the list, and know now much time, effort and cost is involved in each alternative. Do the research beforehand. Prepare a list of options and know what each one costs, and be ready to respond immediately when you get a question or hear a competitive offer from the Trindle negotiator. In split-second negotiating, it helps to have such a menu of services right on your laptop or some other device. It also helps—and this can be done online—to be able to review some of your other customized sets of services delivered to other clients. "For ABC and Associates, I did X, Y, and Z for $abcd . . ." Split-second negotiating means having all of these figures at your fingertips.

Know your client

Research them top to bottom—corporate structure, individuals involved (through Google, LinkedIn, Facebook, and other sources). Observe the photo presentations on their website for your city and other cities; get an idea what they like. Ask questions to learn more about their organization structure. How are decisions made? Do the local managers decide on photo services, or is there a corporate marketing team that makes the call? Once you get the job, who would work with you? You'll have a different relationship if you're working with someone in graphic arts, vs. a marketing department, or with an operations manager or site construction supervisor. Learn the ropes and the internal rules for purchasing photography.

Prepare for the meeting
Know the venue.

Will you have Internet access during the negotiation, so that you can retrieve image samples or previous photo package prices? Will you be able to effectively show your sample photos? Do you need big enlargements, or will there be a projector that you can hook into your laptop? Can you check to make sure the laptop-projector connection works right before the negotiation?

These questions and conceptual frameworks are designed only to get you started. As you might imagine, the "prepare" stage can go quite deep, and it may require a lot of time. But a prepared negotiator has a huge advantage over his or her opponent, and a huge advantage over an unprepared negotiator.

Split-Second Takeaways

1. Figure out what you want from a negotiation.

2. Prepare possible concessions; decide what's essential and what isn't.

3. Research your opponent.

4. Analyze your best alternatives to a negotiated settlement.

Chapter 4
Find Your Negotiating Style

YOU'RE STARTING TO LEARN some of the ground rules of negotiating: Why negotiate, what to negotiate for, how to give and take, and how to prepare. But you're still at the starting point. Why? Because not only do negotiations usually involve complex tasks and complex finances, but they also involve people. Negotiators come from all walks of life—all personalities, all experiences, and all styles. They can be professional negotiators or negotiating professionals (remember the difference?) Of they are people just like you—or many times they're not like you at all.

Part of the preparation process involves understanding and recognizing the different styles, personality styles, and personas of the negotiating world. Not only will you encounter these styles, but you'll most likely adopt one or more of them yourself, depending on the situation, your objectives, and of course, your own personality. And in today's split-second world, you may have to recognize these styles very quickly and through relatively impersonal means—will you be able to recognize an "intimidator" through his or her IM or text messaging style?

In this chapter we will cover six negotiating styles and five negotiating personalities.

Learn the Game
Before you jump into a negotiation, it's important to recognize negotiating styles that attempt to derail your thinking and/or deter you from reaching your

goals. Even more important, you need to know how to play their game, play your game, and defend yourself against them.

The Intimidator

Intimidators employ tactics that don't seem fair to most people because they prey on emotions and prevent you from thinking clearly. They want you to feel as if the negotiation is personal and if something goes wrong it's your fault. They try to stop you from using your head by putting you on the defense in hopes that your bruised ego will prevent you from looking objectively at what is going on.

Is this starting to sound like dealing with psychological warfare? That's exactly what it is. Intimidators take advantage of your human side, focusing less on the business aspect of what you're trying to accomplish and more on the personal side. They ambush you with negativity and sweep you up in a whirlwind of complete chaotic behavior that leaves you wondering what in the world just took place.

Intimidators know their methods are successful because when a person is worked up with anxiety, he'll usually do anything to calm down. That's exactly what the intimidator counts on. He wants you to lose control and give in to his demands just to be done with the stress of the deal. **Remember: a deal made under stress is probably a bad deal.**

▶ Characteristics

If you hear someone shouting and slamming the phone down, you're listening to an intimidator in action. These people are loud, talk fast, make hurried movements, and sometimes use profanity to make a point. They interrupt constantly. Remember—they want to prevent you from thinking clearly so they try to distract and cause you to lose your train of thought, especially when they don't like what they're hearing or they're not getting their way.

Intimidators will walk right into your office and start making demands, not suggestions or requests. Rather than accepting that you're proposing a workable solution benefiting both of you, they'll tell you that they're insulted by an offer of anything less than exactly what they demanded in the first place. They may start yelling again and even throw out a few expletives for extra drama.

In those instances in which the negotiating is being conducted over e-mail, intimidators can present a presence that feels threatening—even if they're thousands of miles away. They can use aggressive language, fill your In Box with strongly worded messages, and threaten dire consequences if their demands aren't met. If all else fails, they can "shout" in an e-mail—type in all caps in an effort to force you to back down and keep you off balance.

Aside from pushing you around, intimidators try to frighten or annoy you with threats. They might threaten to call off the entire negotiation or to bring in someone from upper management or threaten to withdraw their business altogether. Often, these behaviors are bluffs, and you should consider handling them accordingly.

Would You Buy a Used Car from This Man?

Car salespeople often create an intimidating image of their manager to prospective customers to try to scare them out of negotiating an automobile's price. They may convey to the customers the challenge, inconvenience, or difficulty of talking to that manager, complete with body language and a feigned look of anxiety or a negative response. In their word portrait, the manager turns into a combination of Darth Vader and Genghis Khan, and they present themselves as a reasonable force standing between you and this ogre.

Fortunately, you can always call their bluff by asking to talk to the manager yourself. Nine times out of ten, the intimidating picture disappears and the negotiation gets back to where it should be going.

Intimidators may be loud and antagonizing or they may be shrewd manipulators with a barely recognizable yet penetrating insolence. Condescending by nature, these people know how to crawl under your skin and get on your last nerve with just a look, hand gesture, or blink of an eye. They don't intimidate you with scare tactics, but they do it by acting as if they're far above you in every way, making you feel uncomfortable as they patronize both your person and your business sense.

▶ Playing Defense

The best way to defend against intimidators is to avoid stooping to their level. Stay calm, focused, and in control. When the other person starts raising his voice, keep yours at an even tone. Displaying no emotion whatsoever shows them you won't take the bait. You're a professional, and you're there to reach an agreement, not to get into a fight.

In an e-mail exchange with an intimidator, never "shout" or use abusive language. **Remember: anything you write in an e-mail is forever.** Don't create a paper trail (or, if you like, an electronic trail) that your opponent can use against you later. Instead, stay calm, focused, and in control.

Another way to deter intimidators from breaking you down emotionally is to get the focus back on the issues at hand. Ask open-ended questions to avoid brush-offs with simple yes-and-no answers. By forcing them to talk about the real reasons you're both there, they'll cool down and realize you aren't playing their game.

To handle the threat of completely pulling out of the negotiation, first find out if the intimidator is bluffing. If the threat appears to be legitimate, offer up a few of your concessions—but only if it means you'll be able to reach some of your own goals by doing so.

The Flatterer

Like the intimidator, the flatterer focuses more on your emotions than on what solutions you have to offer for reaching a mutual agreement. The difference: the flatterer loads his or her negotiation with insincere remarks meant to be personal and meant to throw you off balance.

The Uses of Flattery

Flattery and intimidation can sometimes be used together as a different type of negotiating style, especially when related to gender. If the two parties involved are a man and a woman, the offending party might use gender-specific flattery ("You're an extremely beautiful woman" or "You look very handsome in that suit") as a way to intimidate the other person, discomfort them, and make them lose focus. I don't recommend you ever use flattery as a way to get an advantage in a negotiation; it can backfire on you very quickly if the other party is on to what you're doing. But I highly recommend that you learn to recognize flattery when it's being employed toward you and that you understand the strategies for countering it.

The flatterer knows that everyone loves to receive compliments, so she takes advantage by buttering up your ego. She may comment on your business style or praise your company, its products, and its CEO. Car salespeople will often tell you how good you look driving in one particular car and how great you could look driving home in another car.

The point of this ego stroking is to make you feel good by appealing to your emotional side in such a way as to give you a false sense of reality. For example, the flatterer will try to make you believe that you have the upper hand and would be doing her a great favor by agreeing to certain concessions.

▶ Characteristics

Since the flatterer tries to make the negotiation personal rather than professional, he may smile a lot and offer up many compliments right away. Throughout the negotiation, he might say something like this: "I know I can't pull one over on you, Bob, that's why I'm giving it to you straight right now." He hopes you'll be so flattered that he recognizes your seasoned negotiating skills that you'll accept it and thank him for being honest with you.

Watch the Faces

Since extreme flattery is a form of dishonesty, it can be a good indicator as to whether the other party plans to fulfill his side of the bargain. Try to recognize speech patterns and facial expressions when the flattering statement is made, and compare what you've noticed to that of the speech patterns and facial expressions that occur each time the other party agrees with one of your requests.

When the other party makes you the main subject of the discussion, it's difficult to stay focused on the details of the issues you're talking about. It's easy to get sucked into all that wonderful praise because the other person is being pleasant and outgoing. (After all, we all like to listen to nice things about ourselves.) Remember that you're there to create agreements that satisfy business goals, not stroke your ego.

▶ Playing Defense

The flatterer, like the intimidator, is an expert at tapping into your emotions. Handle her the same way you handle the intimidator: redirect the focus back to the issues at hand. It's helpful to take notes because it keeps you on track, shows the other party that you mean business, and reinforces the fact that your goal is to achieve successful negotiations. Stay calm and don't let the flattery frustrate you. Shrug off her remarks by asking open-ended questions that force her to talk about the details of the negotiation.

Another way to defend is to change your tone of voice to one of total indifference. Don't use inflections or interject any personality into your speech. By projecting a steely, emotionless image to the other party and refusing to react to the sweet talk, she'll eventually realize that you're not succumbing to the tactics.

If the flattery occurs in e-mails, one way to derail it is to copy a third party on the correspondence, adding something along the lines of "I think in this part of the discussion it might be a good idea to involve my manager. I'm copying her so she knows how our discussions are going."

The Seducer

The seducer, as you can imagine, has lots of charming tricks up his sleeve. He paints a perfect picture for you and describes everything exactly as you want to hear it. But when you get down to the nitty-gritty details, the illusion magically disappears. Suddenly, the ideal image you had in your head when you made your concessions has another side to it, not shown until after he got you to agree with him.

▶ ## Characteristics

The seducer is crafty and unethical and will make attractive offers and concessions to you throughout the negotiating process. Once he has you, he'll reel you in little by little, telling you more of what you want to hear. As soon as you make the commitment, he fills you in on the fine print and swoops in with information like, "You agreed to A but before you can get it you'll need B." And just like that, the deal he's really offering begins to emerge.

The seducer often fails to live up to his part of the deal with reasons like "The paperwork is still being finalized," "My manager hasn't authorized it yet," or "I'm waiting to hear from my lawyer." At a time of split-second deals, he often employs time-delaying tactics. These indications tell you that you might have to get some help on your end, too.

▶ Playing Defense

Protecting yourself from the seducer is simple: don't deal with him. Such manipulation, if not caught in time, can cost you in the long run. You might agree to things you thought were discussed in detail, only to find out about the fine print later. If it's too late and you already made agreements with this person, revisit the negotiation or talk to a lawyer or superior. If you've recognized the signs early on, simply leave the negotiation for other alternatives.

Research is your best friend here. The more you find out about the party you'll be dealing with in negotiations, the better your chances of identifying a seducer early and staying out of his way.

If you decide to continue negotiating with the seducer, be sure you're informed of every detail of the agreements made. Ask questions, and lots of them. Be 100 percent sure you know exactly what's expected of you, and exactly sure what you're getting. Also, take notes. Not only does note-taking help you remember everything said, it lets the seducer know you're paying attention to every word and that you're on to his scheme.

The Complainer

Although the complainer is not as deceitful and unfair as the other negotiating personalities, she can still have a negative effect on your success. In fact, all the complainer really wants is to be heard and to be understood. Once she feels this has been accomplished, she becomes more reasonable and more pleasant to work with.

▶ Characteristics

The complainer can sometimes come across as a *positional* negotiator (see Chapter 2) because she doesn't appear to look past her own needs. It might appear that she doesn't want to budge from her position, but in a way she's really looking for your help.

She'll make statements like, "How can you expect me to give you a free warranty when you're already asking me for a discount?" or "You have no idea how expensive it is for production to make the kinds of changes you're asking for." If you listen closely, there's a cry for help couched in those sentences.

When the complainer begins statements with "How can you" and "You have no idea," she really wants you to ask her to explain what she means. For example, you would ask, "What is preventing you from giving me both a free warranty and a discount?" and "How expensive would it be for production to make these changes?" The complainer is filled with anxiety over your requests and needs you to hear her out.

▶ Playing Defense

You'll need a good ear and an empathetic heart to guard against the complainer. If you handle the situation with the right amount of patience and understanding, you may find that she's not really a positional negotiator at all, and a win-win is in sight. In addition to listening, it helps to be knowledgeable about her situation. Then you can frame your response along the lines of, "Well, after looking at your last quarter's sales numbers, which were posted online, I can certainly understand . . ."

As soon as the complainer starts voicing her concerns, let her have free reign of the airwaves. Hear every word she has to say, and encourage her to say more. Nod, make eye contact, and use hand gestures to let her know you are really listening to what she has to say. You could even plug in an "I see" or a "That's understandable" as a verbal acknowledgement and a sign of active listening. Your good ear will do wonders because once it's all let out, the burden is lifted and she'll relax—and play into your needs.

Active Listening

Your job doesn't end at listening. Listen actively. Paraphrase a few of the complainer's key points to show empathy and correct understanding of her situation. If you're conducting the conversation by e-mail, repeat portions of her e-mail when you reply to show you've read and understood the entire message.

Once finished listening to the complainer's viewpoint, ask more questions to slowly get back to the details of the negotiation. You might even offer a concession, a small one saved for later, or one that you can afford to be a little flexible with. Show the complainer that you see her point and will try to make every effort to make the negotiation just as successful for her as you want it to be for yourself—a win-win.

The Arguer

An arguer argues main points or nitpicks smaller points throughout the negotiation. An opponent may start out with this approach or turn into an arguer midstream in the negotiation.

▶ Characteristics

The arguer can easily be spotted by how often he debates your issues and requests. Let's face it: Negotiating can be all about debating and arguing with the other side until you feel like you've won. But it's important to know what's worth arguing for and what isn't.

Here's a good rule of thumb. Ask yourself or the other party to explain the main concern of an argument. Focus on resolving that issue first, but be aware of any meaningless arguments that pop up along the way. It's easy to get so caught up in trying to prove a point by winning smaller, insignificant arguments while the real issue at hand is often lost along the way. Some arguers are motivated by distraction, others by the need to score small victories along the way. Just keep asking yourself: Do you want to be right? Or do you want to win? Often you can do both, but in many situations, being right at the expense of winning ultimately means you'll win the battle but lose the war.

▶ **Playing Defense**

The arguer can pounce on your every move toward progress in order to stall the negotiation and buy more time for his case, or to prove his ability to win something. Use the agenda created before the meeting to remind him that you're on a schedule and you'd like to stick to it so that everything on the list is covered. Ignoring aimless arguments by reacting to only the important ones is another defense.

Give Yourself a Break

To handle this type of situation, some negotiators will take a break. Getting away gives room to clear their minds and re-energize. When they re-enter the room they can start fresh and perhaps begin to resolve different issues instead of tackling the problem ones right away.

If the arguer still shows no sign of playing fair, tell him he's approaching your danger zone and that you're ready to walk. Sometimes just checking your watch, shutting your laptop, checking for text messages, getting your papers organized and/or gathering your belongings gets the message across.

The Logical Thinker

The logical thinker, reasonable though she may be, tends to overanalyze issues by lingering on them too long. She'll bring up valid points, which you might acknowledge but might not necessarily agree with. If you don't agree with them, she'll probe your reasons why until you've explained them thirty times, and then probe some more.

The logical thinker is extremely focused and insightful, and can support her beliefs with hard evidence and sound reasoning; she may not be able to understand—or *want* to understand—your reasons for disagreement.

▶ **Characteristics**

The logical thinker is a skeptic and is notorious for excessive questioning. However, her questions are not the frivolous "why" questions—they are specifically designed inquiries aimed at drawing conclusions, testing the validity of statements, weeding out inaccuracies, and evaluating information. She may be trying to gain power by tripping you up along the way.

▶ **Playing Defense**

The best defense against the logical thinker is to make every statement clear and backed up by sound research. Don't use convoluted language or statistics and facts you can't support. Be mindful that every person who asks a question isn't employing the logical thinker style of negotiating. It's when the questions keep coming, one after another, that you know you're dealing with a logical thinker.

Another way to repel the logical thinker's attack is to directly come out and ask, "What is it I can help you understand? What part of this doesn't make sense to you right now?" Keeping it simple and direct deflects the generation of more questions.

Negotiating Personalities

So far in this chapter, we've discussed negotiating styles—which, not surprisingly, are a function of an individual's personality. Negotiating personalities are building blocks of one's negotiating style, and understanding the personality will help you unlock the style. Understanding your own personality and how it drives you will also help you determine your own negotiating style. Since successful negotiating involves knowing as much as you can about your counterpart, these clues are invaluable, and can help you assess and predict the other party's behavior throughout the negotiation.

We will cover five negotiating personalities on the following pages.

Aggressive and Dominating

An aggressive negotiator has the following familiar personality traits:

- Demanding
- Pushy
- Bossy
- Self-centered
- Controlling
- Defensive
- Competitive
- Persistent
- Power junkie (enjoys power and respects people in power)
- Forceful
- Challenging
- Disdainful of weakness
- Rude
- Vengeful
- Easily angered
- Dominant
- Intimidating
- Ambitious
- Successful
- Impatient
- Shrewd
- Fast learning

These negotiators act fast and don't want to spend any more time with you than necessary. They're usually busy, rarely with time for lunch, and they thrive in a fast-paced work environment—in fact, precisely the kind of split-second atmosphere for which this book is preparing you. Before meeting with them, have all the facts prepared, and be ready for a speedy discussion. They have no patience and will try to rush you along every chance they get. It's difficult to get control over the discussion with this personality type.

Who's a Type A?

Aggressive personality types are said to have a "Type A" personality because of their high-speed way of life. They are achievers and often motivated by power; they work constantly and are never satisfied with how much they're able to achieve.

▶ **Objectives**

Not only do these negotiators want to win at all costs, they want to win as much as they can and give as little as possible. Victory is their main goal, and they're used to getting their own way. They may adopt a positional negotiating style, caring little for how you fare in the deal. Because they handle each encounter with a ruthless approach, they're easily riled up and tend to show no mercy.

▶ **Common Behaviors**

During a negotiation, aggressive types make quick decisions and will try to get you to do the same. They never seem to have time for you, so they don't tolerate hesitation or thoughtful reflection. Threats and personal attacks, whether in person or by e-mail, may be part of their game, and they will be difficult to deal with if you are an emotional or sensitive person.

▶ **Playing Defense**

"Fight fire with fire" may be one tactic—or you can try to slow them down by being cool, calm, and matter-of-fact. Sticking to—and pinning them to—a well-structured agenda can also help. Turning the floor over, or having the floor turned over to someone else in the room or on the call can also help.

Passive and Submissive

This personality is the exact opposite of the aggressive personality. Submissive negotiators tend to exhibit the following characteristics:

- Nice, Friendly
- Considerate
- Insecure
- Uncomfortable with conflict
- Fear not being liked
- Sensitive
- Shy
- Introverted
- Good listener
- Loner
- Calm
- Reserved
- Avoid being the center of attention
- Prefer to work alone or with few people rather than in groups
- Obedient
- Quiet

Naturally, this personality type has difficulty with aggressive negotiators. Because submissive personalities are more focused on pleasing other people, others often take advantage of them.

Be Firm and Resolute

If you are submissive and absolutely have to negotiate with an aggressive personality, you'll need to desensitize yourself before you begin. Resolve to be firm, focused, and determined to have your goals met.

▶ **Objectives**

Submissive negotiators want others to like them. They'll do whatever they can to make the other party happy, even if it means giving up extra concessions or letting the other party renege on one of theirs. They are well suited to win-win negotiations, but they may be inclined to give up too much too early.

▶ Common Behaviors

These people are the relationship-savers of a negotiation. They really can't bear the thought of someone being upset with them or showing disapproval of their actions. When this happens, they think they've hurt the other person's feelings and immediately begin working on solutions that mend the broken relationship.

Submissive personalities seldom take control of the negotiation. They don't like the limelight, and they're more comfortable following than leading. Consequently, they usually end up agreeing to everyone else's ideas, and they let the other party make all the decisions of the final agreement. They don't want to cause chaos or disturb the peace, so they rarely speak out of turn or voice their thoughts and opinions.

▶ Playing Defense

No defense against such people is required. You may have to work to draw out their true needs or agenda. The key to this personality type is to do what's needed to preserve the relationship—and to get invited back for a subsequent negotiation. Although you may be tempted to take advantage of them to get more than they should give, resist doing this. You want to develop a long-term relationship with this person, and that won't be helped by pushing them into an obviously unfavorable deal during your first negotiation.

Logical and Analytical

Analytical people can be recognized by the following traits:

- Probing
- Apprehensive
- Mistrusting
- Fact-checker
- Thoughtful
- Organized
- Prepared

- Thinker
- Always early or on time
- Even-keeled
- Thrive on information
- Thorough with details
- Take time with decisions
- Insensitive
- Logical
- Fair
- Firm
- Critical

Logical negotiators must have all the facts, details, and information to understand what's taking place at the negotiating table. Instead of rushing ahead, they want to first be prepared. They want to know what to expect before it happens so they can take the necessary steps to prepare for it.

▶ **Objectives**

Analyzers like to problem-solve and seek deeper understanding of what they already know. They want to walk away from the negotiation feeling like they accomplished something. To achieve their goal, they must first be successful in reaching secondary goals, something that involves a careful review of available information, a logical approach to the solution, and an explanation of why it all works.

▶ **Common Behaviors**

Expect logical personalities to walk into the meeting room with an armful of data. At some point during the discussion, you'll inevitably feel like you're under a microscope being closely examined and scrutinized. The opponent is looking for errors in your argument, flaws with your concessions, and inconsistencies in your solutions. While this may come across as overcritical behavior, remember that analyzers need to know that they've covered all bases before making a decision. It helps if you've got your PC or BlackBerry handy so you can counter their data with information of your own.

Keep Up the Pressure

Analytical negotiators often take a long time to make decisions; they always feel like there's one more element they have yet to explore. Because of this, you'll need to give them a little push during closing or you'll be there for days waiting for them to approve the final agreement.

▶ **Playing Defense**

Be prepared. When possible, have documentation to back up your justifications for certain concessions. Graphs, charts, slides, and reports are helpful too. Also, rethink your strategy if it involves bluffing, stretching the truth, or skewing the facts—you can bet that somewhere in that stack of papers lies the truth. Expect a lot of questions. Though it may feel like you're on trial at first, know that this is how analyzers gather the information they need to make decisions. Be aware of how you answer them, too; they tend to be suspicious of a short, quick response, especially if it doesn't answer their question directly.

Friendly and Collaborative

The collaborative negotiator is easy to recognize from the following traits:

- Fair
- Courteous
- Empathetic
- Considerate
- Appreciative
- Understanding

- Honest
- Tactful
- Warm
- Friendly
- Successful
- Open-minded
- Resourceful
- Sincere
- Patient
- General concern for others
- Ability to employ creative thinking techniques
- Flexible
- Sensitive
- Tolerant
- Great character and integrity

These ideal negotiators possess the principles needed to reach win-win solutions. They understand that a negotiation is not a battle, but rather an opportunity to attain mutual success with the least amount of resistance and negativity.

▶ Objectives

Collaborators are concerned with working toward results that allow everyone to walk away from the table quickly and in agreement. They also want to build trust and encourage and develop solid relationships for the future. Tactics include learning as much as possible about the other person and his objectives so that the desired outcome can be achieved.

▶ Common Behaviors

Count your blessings if you're ever in the position of negotiating with a collaborator. You'll know right away by the warm smile, friendly handshake, and overall jovial bearing. At the same time, these negotiators display a keen business sense and make you feel like you're about to be part of something wonderful.

Working with Others

When you work with a collaborator, who directs the discussion and brings up new issues?

Once the discussion begins, ideas, thoughts, and concerns flow back and forth in a natural, easygoing current. The atmosphere is comfortable because collaborators have mastered the art of listening, and they invite you to share anything with them. You can expect this personality type to remain calm, professional, and active in searching for the best outcome.

▶ Playing Defense

Again, no "defense" is really necessary; the goal should be to collaborate with them and to preserve and build the long-term relationship. Above all, be honest in your dealings with them. They'll appreciate it, and it will lead to a consistent search for win-win solutions for both of you.

Evasive and Uncooperative

These negotiators have the following traits:

- Insecure
- Fearful
- Careful
- Play it safe
- Don't like confrontation
- Introverted
- Timid
- Calm
- Reserved

- Procrastinator
- Nonresponsive
- Cold
- Pessimistic
- Easily embarrassed
- Indifferent
- Passive-aggressive

Evasive, uncooperative negotiators deal with issues by disregarding them altogether. It's not that they don't want to succeed; they either don't know how to or are reluctant to approach the issues out of disinterest or weakness, or they are engaged in a power play to control the situation by not offering much or responding much (classic "passive-aggressive" behavior.)

▶ **Objectives**

The goals of these negotiators are either to endure the negotiation without losing, or to win by controlling with silence. They aspire to the first goal out of insecurity, lack of knowledge about the subject, or anything else that may make them feel too uncomfortable to participate in the discussion. Lack of cooperation and silence for them are survival techniques to avoid saying anything that might cause further discussion of the issues. Note, though, that passive-aggression can be used by negotiators to control the situation by not saying or offering much and forcing initiatives onto the other party.

▶ **Common Behaviors**

It's easy to get frustrated with this negotiating type because they're always postponing the discussion of subjects that might cause a debate or withholding or delaying critical information. As a result of putting everything off, a lot of unresolved issues arise, and you get the feeling that nothing much is being accomplished. In addition, communication begins to break down because the negotiators continue to avoid those same issues when they resurface later. It's a difficult cycle to break once it begins because the nature of this type of personality is to avoid tension, confrontation, aggressiveness, anger . . . in fact any emotion they perceive as "negative."

▶ **Playing Defense**

This personality type presents problems, and it's up to you to diagnose their real cause. If the driver is insecurity, try to draw the negotiators out of their shell by reaching out to them and helping them overcome their fear. If your opponent is passive-aggressive, focus on the need to get the task done; make a few concessions to show that they have control, but don't withhold information. If you keep crucial data to yourself, information that could lead to a successful outcome for both parties, you're just keeping the cycle going, and that's to no one's benefit.

Expressive and Communicative

Expressive negotiators have the following traits:

- Playful
- Spontaneous
- Energetic
- Talkative
- Sociable
- Charming
- Self-involved
- A "people person"
- Open
- Easily distracted
- Short attention span
- Enthusiastic
- Think out loud
- Extrovert
- Like being the center of attention

- Ambitiouc
- Not a good listener
- Like to be reassured

These negotiators are generally very animated and convey a fun-loving attitude in most situations. They enjoy their work, crave attention, and thrive on rapport. They want to get the negotiation done, feel like they've won, and believe they've entertained you along the way.

▶ Objectives

Aside from becoming your new best friend, the main goal of expressive negotiators is to see how much they can get out of the deal by using their social skills and optimism. When you reject one of their offers, they tend to take it personally. How could the discussion be about anything other than them? They spent a lot of time hamming it up with you, and they expect to be rewarded!

▶ Common Behaviors

There's no denying that expressive negotiators have upbeat personalities that can be a breath of fresh air in the conference room or in an e-mail conversation. Instead of conducting business in a stuffy, even-mannered tone, they turn the negotiation into a social function. They may jump from one topic to the next and may be hard to pin down on a particular product. At times they may not let you get a word in edgewise.

▶ Playing Defense

Allow them to build rapport, and return the favor. Then, try to keep the negotiation on task with well-timed questions and a focus on the agenda. Don't let them jump around, and don't let them do too much schmoozing. Avoid being too consumed by their charm.

Case Study:
Dealing with Difficult People

At RGB Photographic, your discussions with Trindle and Trundle Associates are moving into high gear. You've prepared your list of demands and possible concessions; you know what your goal is (become Trindle's exclusive Shady City photographer) and how to recognize it when you reach it. You have also listed your secondary goals and you've extensively researched Trindle and Trundle to make sure you know how their organization makes decisions. Finally, you've prepared the venue for the meeting.

Now the day is at hand. You walk into the meeting, shake hands, make some small talk, take a sip from your coffee cup, and click on your first PowerPoint slide to start your presentation.

Then it comes; a voice from somewhere in the room that you recognize as Trindle's CEO: "I don't know why we're having this discussion. Frankly, I don't see what you can do for us that your competitors can't do better."

This is split-second negotiating, so you'll have to think on your feet. Clearly you've run up against an intimidator, someone whose negotiating style is to be overbearing and to establish dominance in the room. As you try to move forward with your presentation, your first impression is confirmed. He interrupts you every few minutes, contradicting what you say, questioning your numbers, and suggesting that Trindle is doing you an enormous favor by even listening to you.

There's no time to regroup or start your presentation over. You're going to have to cope with this issue here and now. You keep your voice calm and your body language minimal. There's no reason to give this guy the impression he's upsetting you. You need, above all, to defuse the situation and get the discussion back on track.

So you do what he doesn't expect. You throw the ball back to him.

"I hear what you're saying," you reply calmly. "Just for clarity's sake, would you explain what photographic services you're getting from the competition? Then I'll show you how I believe RGB can beat those services, both in price and in scope."

Now you've forced him to focus on specifics, and the discussion moves away from emotion (the plane on which the intimidator works best) and back to the level of facts and figures. Things are back to where they should be.

Split-Second Takeaways

1. Among negotiating styles are: the Intimidator, the Flatterer, the Seducer, the Complainer, the Arguer, and the Logical Thinker.

2. Negotiating personalities include: Aggressive, Passive, Logical, Friendly, Uncooperative, and Communicative.

Chapter 5
Developing a Tactical Toolkit

NOW IT'S TIME TO move on from the more strategic and stylistic considerations of negotiation to those "day of the show" tactics, techniques, tricks, role-playing, and ploys used by experienced negotiators. As you might suspect from our discussion in the previous chapter, these tactics are often designed to influence or manipulate opponents by toying with their emotions. While it's not advisable to use many of the ploys described in this chapter to achieve win-win success, knowing how to recognize them helps you avoid falling for these tricks.

Maintain Professional Integrity

As mentioned earlier in this book, the best negotiation strategies proceed from a win-win goal; that is, your aim should be to strike a deal that benefits both of you. This isn't always possible—after all, some deals are more advantageous to one party than the other—but I strongly caution you against doing or saying anything in a negotiation that could be construed as dishonest. It might get you a momentary advantage, but in the long run it will ruin your reputation and make it far more difficult to do business.

In this age of instant communication, it's as well to remember how fast and how widely negative stories can spread. The best way to avoid that is not to give anyone cause to circulate such rumors.

In "split-second" negotiating mode, it's even more important to recognize and deal with these tactics and ploys in real time. You won't have a lot of spare time to carefully study and analyze what the other party is up to. Instead, you'll have to know negotiating types and their tactics so well that you can instinctively recognize them when they're being deployed. This chapter explores some of the most common tactics and role plays used during negotiations and makes suggestions about how to counter them.

Good Cop/Bad Cop

Easily recognized in most cases, the good cop/bad cop ploy is an entertaining display of two people on the same team who play opposite roles in an effort to distort your perception and control your emotions. The bad cop is the disagreeable negotiator, always unreasonable, irritable, and angry. The good cop, on the other hand, is calm and helpful, the peacemaker or collaborator who interjects to tell the abrasive personality to ease up a little bit, thus creating the impression of helping you.

Surely you've viewed this scene on a television show or in a movie. The bad cop interrogates the murder suspect by screaming, threatening, and bullying him, then storms out of the interrogation room only to be replaced by the good cop who befriends the suspect by offering him cigarettes, being nice to him, and promising to help him out of the situation he's in if he just reveals where the murder weapon is or where the body is buried.

You may have also witnessed this ploy at the car dealership. The salesperson will play the good cop and his manager, who is never seen, plays the bad cop who won't let the salesperson make any concessions. The salesperson will go back and forth to his manager's office and always comes back saying he did everything he could to get what you wanted, but the manager refused to budge.

Working Together as a Team

As you can see, this tag-team approach is a combination of the intimidator and collaborator or seducer (see Chapter 4) working together to control the opponent's mental state. While one causes fear, anxiety, and stress, the other serves to relieve the person of his worries and offer greater hope for success.

When you encounter this duo during negotiations, the bad cop will attempt to intimidate you and is sure to reject every offer you make—he may even rush out of the room in a huff. The good guy will then come in to the rescue and let you know he's on your side. Because this technique is not difficult to identify, you'll be able to counter it right away. There are several ways:

- Tell them that from here on out you want to negotiate with the good cop only.
- Call them on it. Ask how long they plan to put on the good cop/bad cop performance for you.
- Play along. Pretend to be alarmed by their statements, then call off the negotiation all together. You'll find that they quickly change tactics if there's a chance of losing altogether what they want to gain in the negotiation.
- Bring your own bad cop into it. Tell them you'd be more than happy to agree to their demands, but you have a supervisor who never bends the rules. Be creative with how rough and tough you make out your bad cop to be.
- Tell the good cop you'd like to speak to him privately. Once alone, tell him you're about to walk away from this negotiation because of the bad cop's behavior and lack of professionalism. Give him or her a five-minute break to discuss with the bad cop.
- Remember to employ one of these counters as soon as you see the pattern. Getting the bad cop out of the picture early in the game allows the rest of the negotiation to progress.

Shills and Decoys

Shills are people or items that act as bait to lure customers. Shills are used in auctions, and on occasion in casinos. Managers may have casino employees pose as customers stationed at slot machines, winning jackpot after jackpot, or at blackjack tables, having fun and showing their excitement with whoops, clapping, and laughter. The plan, of course, is to draw customers into the excitement. When a negotiator announces a hot deal or a new product in a negotiation or on a website he may be employing a shill.

Decoys divert attention away from the real issues. In a negotiation, a decoy may manifest itself in the form of a change of subject away from the main interest or topic of the negotiation. A decoy may be used in a defensive position, for instance, when you bring up a prior delivery problem or issue, which may not have really been a problem but it is played up to get the opponent to give you a concession.

Deliberate Decoys

Some decoys are set up deliberately. A contractor, for example, might intentionally come up with a small estimation "error" in your favor and use it as leverage against you. He might point it out but then suggest that it means you should give something up—something he wants much more than what he gave you. In this case, if you give him a concession you normally wouldn't have, you've been tricked because the estimate was actually not in error. It was something he intended to give up all along.

"Forgive me, I mistakenly included the floor mats in the total out-the-door car price" might get you to feel good about the deal, feel bad for the salesman, and get you to stop the negotiation right there. But you're being had.

The best way to defend against shills and decoys is, first, to recognize them, then to keep the focus on the real issues of the negotiation.

The Straw-Man Technique

Straw-man techniques are used to make the other party believe something is valuable when it really isn't. Your opponent makes a concession that appears important, even if that's not actually the case.

Suppose that during the negotiation process of buying a house you decide you want to purchase the washer and dryer as part of the deal. The sellers recognize this as an opportunity: they were planning to buy a new washer and dryer anyway, and they weren't planning to take the old ones with them. But since they now know you want them, they've got some additional bargaining power. Rather than simply say, "Sure. We didn't want to take them with us anyway," they display concern and contemplation. It's obviously a wrench for them to let these machines go . . . but . . . well, maybe if you're willing to throw in a couple hundred extra toward their closing costs. They've made an apparent concession *to* you, but in fact they've used something they didn't care about to extract a concession *from* you.

What Is Bundling?

Bundling is a clever way of getting the other party to make two or more concessions at once by clumping them together so they seem contingent upon each other. For example, when you're fully committed to all the agreements made, and all the papers have been signed, suddenly the other party asks you to pay certain fees. You'll often agree since everything has been settled already.

Another straw-man tactic is the use of an unnecessary delay to trade for something else of value. For example, the other party will tell you that they need more time to sleep on an issue. Then they offer to give you a decision right away—in exchange for a concession. They really don't need the extra time to make up their minds—it's a straw man. This is an especially common one in the kind of high-speed negotiation we've been talking about, because your opponent can use your desire for a speedy resolution against you.

One defense against the straw-man tactic is to let the other party make all the offers first. This allows you to ask questions revealing their needs and concerns, and leaves you in a position to use the straw-man tactic on them. "You need more time to decide? How can I help you reach the decision more quickly?" Another method is to ask questions about motives and call their bluff when you can. "Were you really planning to take that old washer and dryer to the new house? It's looking kind of old and outdated in that avocado green, isn't it? And it's so old I can't imagine it works all that well. Hardly worthwhile to spend the expense of hauling it over to the new place."

Taken by Surprise

An unexpected twist in the negotiation can throw you off guard or switch you from relying on facts to reacting out of emotions. In an instant, the negotiator brings up new information or displays a new behavior hoping to bring an emotional response or reaction from you. The reason is threefold.

First, he wants to break your concentration and take focus from your objectives and achieving your goals. A sudden fit of anger, for example, can be intended to stir up your emotions. The hope may be that you respond with fear, shock, or frustration. If you take the bait and respond with an equal amount of anger, it may be a while before you get back to discussing the issues at hand.

Second, the opponent anticipates your negotiation efforts will be thrown off-kilter once you let your guard down and give him an emotional response. If, for example, you react with anger, you may say something that can be used against you later to deflate your character or prove one of his points.

Lastly, the negotiator tries to get an emotionally driven concession you previously did not want to give up.

Luckily, there are several ways to counter this assault on your emotions:

- Do not react. Since that's exactly what the other party is hoping for, simply do not give in to the ploy. Stay calm and show your professionalism.
- Take a break. Give yourself time to let the new information sink in or to cool off.

- Ask for details. Learn as much as you can about the new information you've just been given, and determine if it's truly something to be worried about.
- Call for help. If the other party introduces new information to the negotiation and you're not prepared to handle it, convene with your team to discuss how to handle the new information.

Don't Be Surprised

Some negotiators are known for using surprise tactics. If you know that ahead of time, mentally prepare yourself for it by preparing to redirect the focus back to the negotiation. This will help you remain unaffected by the other party's attempts to disrupt your composure.

Sometimes the surprise can be that a party member, usually a supervisor, is unable to attend one of the meetings so he sends another person to take his place. This person then tries to tire you out by asking you to bring him up to speed on the negotiation and to answer all his questions about a particular issue. By prodding you for the same information over and over again, he's hoping to wear you out so you'll just give in to his concessions without putting up a fight.

The obvious defense is to maintain your composure, and to stay focused on the goals and main points of the negotiation. If necessary you can suggest waiting until the original negotiator is available again (though if the negotiations are being conducted quickly, you probably won't have time to do this).

Add-ons and Nibbling

These two tactics are a bigger deal than their names suggest. An add-on is a small concession that a negotiator asks for and adds to the end of a larger concession that's already being discussed. For example, "I'll buy your product if you throw in a free one-year warranty."

If you never intended to give the free warranty, do not feel pressured to do so now. Similarly, do not feel as if you were "taken" if you do decide to agree to the concession; make sure it's something you feel comfortable giving to the other party.

"Nibbling" describes the manner in which a negotiator will ask for "one last thing" after reaching a mutually beneficial agreement. Such negotiators are rarely satisfied with the agreements that have been made; they always must ask for another concession, and another, and another. They may say, "Forgot to ask before" or "One other thing," or "Can we make a change or two?"

As with most ploys, the way to play defense is to confront them head on. If you notice that the negotiator is continuously asking for extras, especially after everything has been finalized, ask if she's happy with the deal the way it is. If she says yes, then tell her you feel that a fair settlement has been made and you see no reason to make more changes. If she doesn't back down, ask if you can make some changes as well.

Some Concessions Are More Equal Than Others

Just because it sounds like the negotiator is asking for a small concession doesn't mean the concession is small. Before agreeing to his request, determine if doing so will help you achieve your goals and objectives.

Additional Techniques

Here are a few other common negotiating tricks and ploys to watch out for:

- *Funny money*. This is real money presented in a way that makes it less real. When gambling, you exchange hundred-dollar bills for chips, a tactic casinos employ to make customers feel like they're not gambling with "real" money—when in fact that's exactly what they're doing. In negotiating, the other party may use funny money—like talking in percentages or points instead of dollars—to shift your focus away from cost or price.

- *Red herring.* A person makes a phony demand, only to trade it off later for another one. For example, if the real objective is to get you to agree to a 20 percent discount on production fees, the other party might start by demanding something bigger, like a free three-year service warranty. When you decline the red-herring warranty request the opponent then comes back for the 20 percent discount.

- *Low balling.* This tactic is used primarily in the retail industry. When comparison-shopping for a computer, for example, one retailer might tell you he can sell it for under a specified dollar amount—much lower than the competitors' prices. After researching several stores and discovering higher prices, you return to the first store only to be refused and given a litany of excuses—the salesperson's manager won't approve the price, the price was a one-time offer, the figure was miscalculated, or the salesperson who gave you the quote is not working today.

- *Flinching.* Suppose the other party threw a dollar amount out there but didn't really expect you to go along with it. Why would he suggest it if he didn't think you'd agree to it? Because he wants to see what kind of reaction you give him. If you have no reaction, he might assume that getting the amount is a possibility. However, if you gasped in shock or put your hands on your cheeks and dropped your jaw, he'll drop his price because it's obvious you're not happy with the price. (The reaction doesn't have to be visual; he can learn a lot from the tone and word choice of your e-mail response.) When the other party gives you an outrageous dollar amount, don't hold your feelings back. Instead, use flinching to convey your disagreement with the number he has given you. Don't forget—flinching is also effective on the telephone and today's other media devices.

- *Crunch.* The negotiator uses this tactic to make you doubt your position by rejecting your entire offer, using terms like, "You'll have to do much better than that" and "That's just not good enough for me." Intimidators specialize in this sort of tactic. The negotiator using this method is never satisfied and may try to make you feel fortunate to get another chance at making a different offer. Since she'll never give you reasons why your offer wasn't good enough, you'll need to ask for details about why it seems so unreasonable. In truth, once you get into the nitty-gritty of the offer, you'll find that many of the objections to it disappear quickly.

- *Escalation.* Escalation occurs when you find yourself in the fortunate position of having enough deal "leverage" to get more out of an agreement than already settled upon. The opponent is already so emotionally involved that he doesn't want to back out of the deal. You can use this to your advantage—but keep the long-term relationship in mind. People who "lose" negotiations tend to remember those losses.

- *Bogey.* A bogey is used as a scapegoat when trying to explain the inflexibility of the other party. For example, the negotiator will blame a third party, for example her manager, for why she cannot come down in the cost of production fees. When you detect a bogey, ask to speak to or learn more about the bogey. Remember, you want to negotiate with the person who has the authority to make and accept concessions.

When You're the Underdog

Negotiating power is dependent on a number of components, all of which work together to create the leverage you can use during the negotiating process. Normally, both sides have more or less equal bargaining power; it's common to perceive that one side has more of it than the other. Both sides typically have strengths and weaknesses that can be used to their advantage to create win-win solutions that work around the table.

That all said, sometimes you will find yourself in a position of unequal power or leverage. It's important to learn some tactics for handling such a situation, and handling it quickly in this split-second world.

Suppose the other party has a prestigious reputation, is a long-acknowledged expert on the topic, has superior negotiating skills, and has a stellar team backing him up. You have none of these advantages, making you the underdog in the negotiations. You can still do well, but you'll need to put more research and time and determination into the negotiation.

First, it's important to recognize the situation and not be intimidated by those credentials. Preparation and a conscious adherence to good negotiating techniques will help.

As you go through the preparation stage, figure out of where you can acquire leverage. Figure out where you can give a unique value proposition, one different from the competition. That will require a careful inventory of your own capabilities and those of the competition.

Be Confident

Your goal is to walk into the negotiation as if you couldn't possibly fail. Take inventory of your assets, and toughen up your negotiation skills to build up your confidence level.

▶ How to Build More Leverage

Timing and deadlines, discussed in Chapter 8, can be used to your benefit if the other party is under strict limitations or under contract to deliver goods and services at a specified date and time. If you have a concession that advantageously impacts the other party's timeline, your offer will become attractive.

Likewise, try to predict what issues your counterpart will be most interested in:

- Money
- Profitability
- Reputation
- Service
- Protection

Look for concessions that fall into these categories, and use them to appeal to the other party's most imperative goals and his means of reaching them. If you sense he's taking advantage of your underdog position, remind him that you're well aware of the leverage you have by focusing his attention on how what you have to offer fits into the above points.

No matter how unpleasant the other party might be to work with, using status as an excuse to be rude, belittling, uncompromising, or impatient, you shouldn't cave in. If you do, you'll only confirm assumptions about your weakness, and the entire negotiation will go downhill from there. Instead, stand up for yourself and let it be known that you won't be steamrolled. Your counterpart will take you more seriously and will have more respect for you in the long run.

▶ Master Your Field

If lack of knowledge about the issues makes you the underdog, take it upon yourself to bridge the gap. Do some quick research. Hit the Internet. Tap your social and professional network. Learn what you can as quickly as you can, become an "instant expert."

If You're Not Ready Yet

Simply put, if you're not ready to negotiate, don't do it. Maybe you need more time to prepare, or maybe you need more information from the other party; whatever the reason, do not put yourself in a position you'll regret later. Let your counterpart know you're not ready, and if he still persists on beginning, give an exact date you'll be ready so he knows you're not purposely putting it off.

If you need additional information from the other party, ask him to provide this to you. Explain how these details will help you solve the conflict that's preventing you from beginning the negotiation process. Your counterpart should have no problem with your request, and if he does, find out why. The answer you receive could be another important factor for you to consider before making your offer.

If you find yourself in a difficult situation, remember the "win-win" paradigm—you want to win, and the other party deserves to win, too. You should give—and ask for—enough time to prepare to come to the table with a reasonable and equal chance to win. The other party might at first try to use your situation to his or her advantage, but if you persist with your adherence to the win-win principle, they should accommodate it. If they don't, they may not be fit to work with in the long term anyway. Don't be afraid to ask.

Case Study: More RGB Showtime Tactics

Once you've silenced the intimidating CEO of Trindle and Trundle in your pitch to make RGB Photographic its exclusive supplier of photographic services, your challenges aren't over. You may have gotten past one difficult person, but Trindle is still intent on beating down your offer to what it considers a better deal. To match it, you'll have to employ some of the tactics we discussed in this chapter.

We mentioned "good cop/bad cop." Well, unless you want to bring your administrative brother-in-law into the negotiation, you might have to settle for playing both roles. Not really doable—although you can sometimes get away with taking a tougher stance, then backing down a bit to make your opponent feel a bit of a victory.

Still, the good cop/bad cop idea can help you along. You settle on one Trindle executive who's been quieter through the discussion. He seems like a nice guy; maybe he's been assigned to play your friend—

the "good cop" in the story—while the CEO is the "bad cop." If you recognize this at the meeting, or better yet anticipate it beforehand in your pre-negotiation reconnaissance, you can act accordingly. This means catering to the bad cop's needs and objections clearly and directly, while engaging the support of your good-cop opponent throughout. So you start appealing to the good cop for comments and input. It's harder for the CEO now to challenge you, since you're throwing back at him facts and figures supplied by someone on his own side.

You can make the good cop's job easier and better by delivering some new service or cutting a cost or time factor out of the work. Now she's got more ammunition to persuade the bad cop, the CEO, that she knows what's best, and he (the bad cop) may step aside. Whatever you can do to make the more reasonable person in the negotiation look better to the less reasonable one will help.

As you move further into the negotiations, you employ a wider range of tactics. Straw men come into play, and photographers have lots of good ones to throw out. In today's digital era, professional-grade prints cost a song yet are still perceived to be expensive by most clients. You throw in some extras, and you offer to save money by combining their aerial shots with the aerial shots of other clients—you can "reduce the price accordingly" while in reality your aircraft rental cost goes away almost completely—it is absorbed by the other job. The more straw men you throw out there, the more cooperative and supportive of the opponent's needs you appear to be—even though the reality of the straw man is that it isn't much of a concession at all. Trindle and Trundle, for example, is likely to want their photos at their preferred time, not when the airplane or helicopter is up for another client.

Split-Second Takeaways

1. Be able to instinctively recognize common negotiating tactics and styles so you can react swiftly to them.

2. Master your field; become an expert in it.

3. If you're not ready to negotiate, don't.

Chapter 6
A Day at the Theater

IN THIS CHAPTER, WE continue to review the split-second tactics, tricks, and ploys employed by negotiators, important both for you to use at times and also to recognize. However, here we'll shift focus to the more visual and theatric ploys a negotiator might employ. Some of these can still be employed in telephone conversations or over e-mail, but many of them will be most effective if you're discussing your issues face to face.

When you're at the negotiating table, the last person you hope to meet is a full-time actor—someone who's mastered bluffing and other tactics and tricks, using them without being noticed. This chapter shines the spotlight on which actors you can expect to make an appearance—and what you can learn from their behavior. We'll also highlight the more subconscious forms of body language that can tell a lot about a negotiator's intentions and reactions to what is going on in the bargaining.

These theatrics and cues are more obvious in person but should not be ignored in a virtual media-supported negotiation. Aside from the most visual forms of body language, they can be discerned—with some effort—over the phone, e-mail and other media.

Playing Dumb

You, or your opponent, may choose to "play dumb"—that is, to be less informed or prepared than you are—to bring a negotiator in your direction or sometimes, to find out more information along the way. Instead of risking an uncomfortable confrontation by coming right out and asking the question, "Why did your production department fail to meet its yearly quota?" it might be more suitable to ask what the production department's numbers were for the year and how they compared to previous years. The other party will be less defensive about the subject and more willing to explain the decline in numbers.

This tactic may allow you to confirm information you already know. Further, it makes the other person aware that you're privy to his information. If you're taking your car to a certain mechanic for the first time, you can ask a few questions to let the person know you've done your research and are not to be taken advantage of.

Don't Be Fooled by Dumb

If the person you're negotiating with starts to play dumb, don't allow the main issue to be derailed by peripheral information that the other party intends to use against you. Ask him right away if there's a deeper issue he would like to talk about, and try to determine where his questions are going. It may simply be that he needs the information and doesn't have it on hand. Just be aware of incessant digging and suspend it before the discussion plays out more like a trial.

When your counterpart uses the "just play dumb" tactic, you can be certain he's searching for something that will strengthen his confidence in presenting or rebutting a concession or important issue. For example, he might have sensed early on in the discussion that you were bluffing about something. In order to get you to reveal what you're hiding, he'll pretend to be ignorant and ask all sorts of questions relating to his suspicions.

▶ The Socratic Method

One way to tell if the other party is playing dumb is to recognize the signs of the Socratic method, a technique of asking leading questions in order to manipulate the other person into giving a particular response. No matter how many questions you answer, more will follow, until you give an answer the other party finds satisfactory.

Learn from the Master

The Greek philosopher Socrates taught his students how to logically think about and argue the statements they made by engaging them in a philosophical debate, ultimately drawing them into a contradiction of their original statement. By actively participating in the debate, the students learned to think for themselves and eventually could see through the trap of Socrates' questioning.

You can avoid this power tactic by redirecting every question to a main objective, asking how the question pertains to the goals you are both trying to reach. Explain that you don't want to waste time on trivial inquiries that don't lead to solutions. If there are some questions that your counterpart insists on asking, keep your answers short to deflect further questioning.

▶ Diffusing a Tense Situation

When the other party's behavior becomes antagonistic, resist the urge to try the Socratic method on your negotiating counterpart; your attempt at manipulation may backfire. However, it is a good idea to play dumb and to be complimentary. If the other party's competitive spirit is getting the best of him, not to mention getting in the way of progress, a little ego stroking will have a calming effect and allow the discussion to continue in a professional manner. To produce this effect, pretend you don't know much about a particular issue your counterpart wants to discuss, and ask for information about it using open-ended questions. He'll get his ego stroked in the process of "educating" you. Meanwhile, you can think of new ways to proceed.

Don't Let Ego Get in the Way

People who operate from ego alone often confuse confidence with arrogance and a know-it-all attitude. Worse, they then get defensive and try to assert themselves because they feel threatened by the person exuding the confidence. It becomes a vicious circle, and if not defused early, unnecessary conflicts could arise.

Conducting Interrogations

When a negotiator relies on questioning, it's important to try and figure out what kind of information he is really looking for. Questions serve many functions, and not all of them conceal a hidden agenda. Nevertheless, it pays to be on guard. Conversely, if you're the one asking questions, consider formulating them to get better responses. The art of formulating and framing questions, often done on the fly, is important. By learning to recognize various question types, you will be able to put together skillful, suitably targeted questions. Here we will describe *vague, loaded,* and *leading* questions.

▶ Vague Questions

Asking vague questions can prompt unexpected responses because they don't lead to a specific answer. If the other party asks vague questions, it's easy to misinterpret what he really means, and you might give an answer you did not intend to disclose. For example, when answering the question, "That figure isn't accurate, is it?" you might inadvertently reveal that the number is adjustable when you weren't ready to discuss that point yet.

To avoid this, ask the other party to elaborate on his question by being more specific: "Why don't you agree with the figure? Is it too high or too low?" If your counterpart is just digging around for information, get exact details about what he wants to know before you give too much away.

▶ Loaded Questions

A loaded question is more like a judgment wrapped up in a nice package topped off with a carefully tied question mark. It sounds like you are being asked a question, but you are really being led to a conclusion. Usually, the presumptive conclusion is a negative one, such as in the questions, "Is your staff still disorganized?" and "Is your unfair request still on the table?" Either way you answer the question, you're admitting a negative condition.

The way to deflect these attacks is to, once again, ask for clarification or a reframing of the question before answering.

Answer a Question with a Question

If you answer right away, you validate the other person's opinion that your staff is disorganized and your request is unfair. You can instead answer the question with another question. Ask him why he thinks your staff is disorderly and why your request seems unreasonable to him.

▶ Leading Questions

Lawyers use these questions frequently, and when they do, an objection from the opposing lawyer is not slow to follow. A leading question tries to get a specific response, usually to prove the asker's point.

In the courtroom, a leading question is often used to create a dramatic presentation for the jury. The opposing lawyer objects to a leading question because it serves only to trick the witness into saying something out of context. Further, the process is unfair to the witness. The lawyer already knows the answers to the questions he is asking; he knows the script and is acting it out using the witness as his unknowing sidekick.

Examples of a leading question during a negotiation might be, "This price is really high, isn't it?" "Isn't your delivery schedule substantially slower than those of your competitors?" or "Your firm has had a lot of quality control issues in the past, hasn't it?" One feature of many such questions is the subquestion tacked on at the end: "isn't it?" "doesn't it?" "don't you?" and so on. A question that is followed by such a subquestion is often leading.

If you think the other party is using leading questions to prove a point, kindly remind her that you are not on trial and that you would like to save time by discussing only the heart of the issues. Or answer the question as if it had been put in a nonleading manner. "How does your delivery schedule compare to that of your competitors?"

Talking, Talking, and More Talking

A well-balanced discussion involves an equal amount of talking and listening among all parties. All negotiators want to feel that what they're saying is important to the rest of the table. When given the chance, however, some people dominate the conversation or discussion by talking entirely too much. Sometimes this is done intentionally, and sometimes the person doesn't even realize how much he's talking. Either way, excessive talking during a negotiation can throw you off center. By the time the other person finishes speaking, you might have forgotten thoughts you had about certain points that were brought up earlier in the discussion.

Talking Too Much?

If you realize that you've been chattering nonstop, stop talking right then and there. Apologize for controlling the conversation, and give the other party the floor. Acknowledging your mistake (instead of covering it up) will help you regain the respect you might have lost. Likewise, you can politely ask others to "take the conversation into the parking lot" or some such.

▶ Reasons for Rambling

The more aware you become of your counterpart's negotiating style, the more you'll be able to correctly guess what his intentions are and why he behaves in certain ways. As mentioned previously, a rant can be either deliberate or purely accidental. Before you react, use the following guide to determine which behavior is being displayed. A long-winded rant can be either deliberate or accidental:

Deliberate

- Denies the opportunity to interject with comments or questions, even when you signal that you have something to add.
- Shrugs off your comments and questions, or says, "Let's talk about that later."
- Interrupts when it is your turn to speak.

Accidental

- Repeats thoughts, speaks quickly, and uses a lot of run-on sentences; this could be a sign of nervousness and insecurity.
- Makes a lot of jokes and aimless chitchat; although it may seem this person is avoiding the issues, this could be an attempt to make a good impression or to establish rapport.
- Fills silences by talking about more concerns or goals; this person may be uncomfortable with long periods of silence or could be thinking out loud.

The More They Talk, the Less They Say

Some people use talking as a way to compensate for what they lack in leverage or offers. The less they have going for them, the more they feel the need to talk to compensate for their deficiencies.

▶ **Information Overload**

Excessive talking can be used as a tactic to bombard you with so much information that you miss the important points. First, the other party gives you all the pertinent facts up front, and then he delivers a deluge of information that has you trying to focus on too many points. Finally, he concludes with details even further from the issues and facts already discussed. The purpose of this ploy is to overwhelm you with so much data that you forget the questions you had about the real issues, fail to notice erroneous assumptions, and miss the chance to inquire about gray areas.

It can be difficult to get a straight answer from these ramblers. The longer the answer, the harder it becomes to extract the information you need. If necessary, repeat the question until you are clear about the real answer. If the other person tries to evade the question with doublespeak, keep pressing. If you want to know how much her company charges in production fees, don't let her get away with an answer like, "Well, it's usually 10 percent, but it has been 20 percent in the past." As you can see, the question still remains to be answered.

The Importance of Note-Taking

When a person speaks for sixty minutes, we tend to remember only what was said during the last five minutes. The same holds true for someone who speaks for forty-five, thirty, or twenty minutes. Take notes every time you and your counterpart confer to make sure you remember everything said. That includes (especially!) conversations that occur over the telephone. It's often a good idea to send a follow-up e-mail to reiterate the main points of the discussion. ("It was good to speak with you this afternoon, Ms. Smith. As we discussed concerning our agreement for a new sales contract . . .")

A Shouting Match

Most people feel uneasy when someone is yelling at them, and they are embarrassed when other people can hear it, even if they didn't do anything wrong. Shouters know this and use that discomfort to their advantage.

Not everyone shouts for the same reason, so listen carefully to what the other party is saying (or shouting) and pick up on the cues. She might be shouting because she feels threatened or intimidated by your expertise. In this case, you can put her at ease by asking for her advice on a particular issue or by asking her to explain a few things to you. This will give her the self-confidence to carry on with professionalism rather than from a defensive attitude.

Pressure from superiors is another reason that the other party might resort to shouting. He is expected to walk away from the deal with specific concessions or to adhere to a strict deadline. Show empathy to restore his confidence in your desire to produce a win-win outcome.

Don't Shout Back

The worst thing you can do when your counterpart starts shouting at you is to shout back. Doing so gives more reason to continue shouting, and the situation will escalate from there. Instead, calmly tell him to back off, and then shift the focus back to a factual discussion. Your composure and focus on reason rather than emotion will calm him down.

Emotional Outbursts

Negotiators who have become seasoned actors know just when to use their dramatic skills to get what they want. In addition to shouting, they might stage tears, put on an air of unconcern, or try to scare you with threats. Their purpose is to tap into your emotions and control the way you think. It's also a way to see how malleable you are. Can you be easily swayed? Or are you focused?

If the other party can create self-doubt in your mind, he can get you to rethink your position on certain subjects. When you encounter these theatrics, ignore them. Announce that you would like to take a break to give the other party some time to compose herself. You can also offer to postpone the negotiation. This will usually get the message across that you have no intention of giving in to any kind of theatrical performances.

What Kind of Emotional Outbursts Can I Expect?

An explosion of anger is the most common kind of outburst. Sob stories and guilt trips are frequently used to make you believe that the situation is worse than it is. Helplessness creates an uncomfortable situation because the other party wants you to think that he's giving up, and there's only one thing you can do to get him to come back. If you give into this act, he'll only use it again.

Blatant Mistreatment

Abuse comes in many varieties. The intention of the abuser is to wreak havoc on your ego to achieve his own goals. Abusers use personal attacks to gain control. Verbal abuse—in the form of name-calling, foul language, emotional exploitation, manipulation, and cruelty—is intended to shake your self-confidence and well-being.

If you feel you're a victim of abuse, let the other party know that you will not accept that kind of behavior and then walk out. If you don't defend yourself, he will lose respect for you and continue acting offensively toward you.

About Body Language

Sometimes the most important part of a face-to-face or video conversation involves no words at all. Becoming fluent in body language requires time, effort, practice, and application, but it's worth the effort. Body language skills will help you uncover hidden agendas, discover a person's true feelings, gain insight into someone's character, predict reactions, and become aware of your own nonverbal behavior.

Unconscious Behavior

The challenge of reading body language lies in how misleading it can be. It's not an exact science, and many nonverbal cues can be interpreted in numerous ways. Even though there are some standard generalizations, each signal is unique to the person and the context. Most of the time we don't know our bodies are silently and subconsciously communicating with the rest of the world.

Speaking body language is instinctive. People don't consciously move their arms when they speak—it just happens. It's natural for arms to move, feet to tap, and eyes to turn away when engaged in verbal conversation. In fact, it feels very unnatural to carry out these behaviors consciously.

Control Is Everything

The ability to control body language is an important part of being an actor. Good actors really know how to employ this silent language to show how the character is feeling.

It's useful to observe how body language is used in conjunction with speech. After you gain some experience with this, you'll realize that nonverbal cues can either emphasize the spoken words or undermine them. For example, if a person says he's satisfied with your offer, but grips his pen and clenches his fist as he says so, you might ask yourself if he's really unhappy with the offer. To test this assumption, ask a few questions to see if he can open up and tell you how he really feels.

There are literally thousands of nonverbal cues to discover, not to mention thousands of ways to interpret them, and we simply do not have the room to list them all here. The following table covers some of the most common nonverbal cues and their functions.

COMMON NONVERBAL CUES	
BODY LANGUAGE	**POSSIBLE MEANING**
Crossed arms	Defensive, immovable, opposing
Crossed legs, ankles	Competitive, opposing
Clenched hands, strong grip on object	Frustration
Cocked head	Interested, attentive
Covering mouth with hands	Dishonesty
Fidgeting	Apprehensive, unconfident
Finger tapping or drumming	Boredom
Frequent nodding	Eagerness
Hand-steepling (forming church)	Confidence
Hands on hips	Confidence, impatience
Hands on cheek, chin, or glasses	Thinking, examining
Hands on table or desk	Poise
Head in hand	Disinterested, disrespectful
Leaning forward	Enthusiasm
Open arms, hands	Open-minded, approachable
Perpetual eye blinking	Deception
Rubbing nose, forehead	Uptight, confrontational
Side glance	Suspicion
Sitting on edge of seat	Prepared, enthusiastic
Slouching, leaning back	Challenging, rejecting
Throat-clearing	Nervousness, impatience

These basic cues are universal and visible. Most are visible, though a few like throat clearing are auditory and can give information on a phone call, for instance. Not surprisingly, today's electronically connected split-second world has many forms of communication like text or IM where such body language cues are lost altogether.

However, these forms of discussion provide their own cues as to the other person's state of mind.

Many cues are more subtle or are combinations of other cues:

▶ Facial Expressions

Evolution has afforded us the ability to develop a wide range of social behaviors, including the resourcefulness of communicating a message with just a single look. As soon as we meet someone for the first time, we begin sizing him up and immediately try to find clues that allude to his character so we can get a general idea of what kind of person we are dealing with.

The Importance of Facial Expressions

Facial expressions summarize a person's disposition and, because of that, prove to be invaluable tools throughout the course of a negotiation. Some signs to look out for include: raised eyebrows (uncertainty, concern); nose scratching (confusion); widening of the eyes (surprise, disbelief, anxiety); and minor eye squinting (contemplative, questioning).

▶ Vocalization

Your voice is instrumental in expressing how you feel. Tone, tempo, and cadence play as crucial a role as word choice in communication. Use your voice to get your point across more effectively, to get someone's attention, to sooth or calm someone who's upset, or to gain insight into your counterpart's intentions.

Tone is composed of many elements: pitch (high or low frequency), stress (emphasis), and volume (loudness) are the elements you need to monitor. It is used to place importance on certain words, and if not done correctly, your counterpart can totally misread your meaning and emotionality. Consider the following example, where bold face indicates emphasis on a particular word:

- What do you **want**?
- What **do** you want?
- What do **you** want?
- **What** do you want?

Notice how the meaning of each question is changed depending on where the emphasis is? If it's still unclear, read each one out loud with the proper inflection and think about how you would react in each situation.

Speak Softly

Loud tones can be used to get someone's attention or to make a point, but they may sound threatening and filled with anger. Soft, quiet tones make people feel relaxed and safe, but they may also signal weakness and be ignored.

Tempo refers to how fast you speak (rushing through sentences or slow and calculated), while cadence is the rhythm or style of your voice (dull monotone or exciting variations). If your counterpart is speaking too fast, he may be nervous or apprehensive. If his voice drones on without any use of tone or pitch, he may be uninterested or distracted.

The Advantages—and Dangers—of Texting

In today's electronic world, communication can still transcend the actual words used. Text or e-mail messages can have a tone as well—they can be very short and curt and to the point, one word, even. Or they can be friendly and explanatory. Because of the effort to produce these messages, especially text, you shouldn't read too much into terse messages. But still, you can pick up some clues, especially if a person is normally likely to send more friendly messages or deliver friendlier messages in person.

Universal Gestures

A funny thing happened as human beings evolved. All across the board, we somehow managed to develop many of the same gesticulations. There are thousands of books, articles, theories, reports, experiments, and tests—all designed to explain this phenomenon. To illustrate a few of the more fascinating results of this data, let's look at how learned behaviors can influence the success of your negotiations abroad.

▶ Transcending the Language Barrier

No matter how different the human race is among its cultures, beliefs, spoken languages, traditions, and individuals, there are some things we all have in common. At birth, we instinctively know that crying brings comfort; as adults, when we see someone laughing we know they are happy.

Gestures Are Forbidden

As a tourist, you may use pantomime so the natives can understand you, but avoid using gestures if you don't know what they mean to the people in the country you're visiting. For example, the "A-OK" hand signal where the thumb and index finger meet to form a circle, is very offensive in some countries, as is the sign for "We are number one."

Mirroring Your Counterpart

An effective way to build trust with the other party is to repeat his style of speaking, writing, e-mailing, texting, tone of voice, and posture. If done with skill (without seeming to mock the other person), your counterpart will feel as if you understand him, and a foundation for open communication will be established. Because most of us have a tendency to favor one sense over the other, the statements we make reflect this choice and help in determining how to follow the other party's lead. These statements will generally fall into one of three of the following categories: visual attributes, auditory forms, or kinesics.

▶ Visual Attributes

People who prefer to understand their world from a mostly visual perspective respond to color, shapes, graphic design elements, and physical movements. They make statements like, "It seems clear from my point of view" and "I see where you're coming from." Try to relate to these people by using similar statements that incorporate visual elements into the sentence, "It looks good to me."

▶ Auditory Forms

As the title suggests, these people are attuned to a world of sounds. They tend to hear before they see, and they recall memories by first describing the sounds they remember during that moment in time. They are keen on observing tone and the sounds of movement (slamming doors, sighs of frustration). Their statements include, "It sounds good to me," "I hear what you're saying," and "I don't have to listen to this."

▶ Kinesics

Kinesthetic people are very object-oriented. They usually need one to "get a handle on the situation" or "grasp the point you're trying to make." It's easy to pick up on their clues because "in light of" how many times you propose your offer, they just can't seem to "come to grips with it." Is any of this starting to ring a bell?

Reading and Sending Appropriate Signals

As you can see, body language isn't quick and easy. You really need to look at the whole picture to get a true read on someone. And there's always the possibility that you misunderstand something. Reading body language is all guesswork; no one can ever be 100 percent sure about what another person's intentions are. Nevertheless, there are a few techniques that can help you recognize patterns and inconsistencies in the other party as well as within yourself.

The Body Language Litmus Test

At the beginning of a negotiation, you and your counterpart will exchange friendly, chatty rapport as a way of getting to know each other. During this process, get to know his nonverbal personality as well. Look for breathing patterns, nuances, and idiosyncrasies; notice if he smiles a lot, grins, or smirks; try to assess his attitude by listening for tone and watching how often he makes eye contact. Once you've committed these impressions to memory, use them as a reference point once negotiations begin.

Be Happy!

Get your counterpart to talk about something he's happy about—like his significant other, children, pets, or cars. Since he's not pretending to be happy about his favorite things, you can make accurate notes about his body language while he's talking about Scruffy, and look for those cues again later.

Who's Bluffing?

The best way to tell if someone is bluffing during a negotiation is to ask questions. If you recognize nonverbal cues that suggest your counterpart is bluffing, put him to the test by poking around to see what you can dig up. As the previous chapters suggest, information is your most powerful tool, and it usually throws the other party off guard if you ask him to back up his statements.

Take a Look in the Mirror

If you want to be sure you're sending the right signals, videotape yourself giving a couple of speeches (even if it's a birthday speech or toast to your best friend) and review the tape often. You can also ask family members and friends how they perceive your body language. Ultimately, the only sure way to know what you're revealing is to perfect your poker face in front of the mirror and practice using it.

Using and Interpreting Silence

A quote from twentieth-century French composer Claude Debussy sums up the power of silence beautifully: "Music is the silence between the notes." This statement illustrates how important the stillness becomes in relation to how much of an impact the music will deliver.

▶ **It Goes Without Saying**

It's amazing how much a person is willing to reveal when you exercise your right to be quiet. Silence can be an important tool in keeping control of the discussion, or in giving others time to think. Be careful not to use (or tolerate) too much silence—you might come off as "passive-aggressive" and thus untrustworthy, or other talkers with not much to say might chime in just to break the silence.

It's also a great way to give your counterpart a chance to voice something he's been waiting for the right moment to say. He'll appreciate that you're not trying to monopolize the conversation by affording him the opportunity to contribute. Say nothing, and let it all happen. It's that simple.

Another way to use silence to your advantage is to put pressure on the other party. Sometimes it'll be misinterpreted as a bad sign by those who don't know any better, but in the game of "He who speaks first loses," it'll work in your favor when the other party relinquishes his position of power.

Case Study: Listening to Unspoken Language

As a representative of RGB Photographic, you're halfway through your discussions with Trindle and Trundle about becoming their exclusive supplier of photographic services. You've pushed back the attacks of the intimidator, a role played by the company's CEO, and by being aware of the "good cop/bad cop" routine employed in so many negotiations you've been able to play off one executive against another. Through your use of straw men you've made some "concessions" that aren't really significant to you, though they sound big to the other side.

As the discussion continues, you notice that one of Trindle's negotiators is sitting hunched in his chair, silent and apparently half ignoring the discussions swirling around him. His arms are folded and his legs crossed, and he's staring intently at a piece of paper in front of him on which there is a series of doodles—not notes about what's been discussed.

Everything about this man screams "No!" He looks deeply unhappy, as if Trindle were about to jump off a cliff. You aren't the only one watching him; other Trindle negotiators are aware of him as well, and his closed attitude seems to be affecting the discussion, which gradually dies down.

Clearly you're going to have to win over this man. But before considering how you'll do it, you take a quick inventory of your own body language:

- Are your arms or legs crossed?
- Are you meeting others' gazes directly?
- Are you frequently covering your mouth or touching some other facial feature?
- Are you slouching in your chair?

If you've been doing any of these things, you've been sending a clear set of signals to your opponents—just the wrong signals. Remember that you're engaged in win-win negotiation; you want to arrive at an agreement that benefits both RGB and Trindle and Trundle. You're not going to accomplish that if they think you're sullen, resentful, or holding something back.

Right now, having identified a problem by correctly reading body language, you're ready to use whatever tactics are necessary to bring the recalcitrant Trindle executive on board and keep the negotiations moving forward.

Split-Second Takeaways

1. Theatrics are a big part of any negotiation; learn when to use them and when to avoid them.

2. Find out what the other party wants to know.

3. Talking is a key part of any negotiation—but learn when to be quiet.

4. Study body language—yours and your opponent's.

Chapter 7
Avoiding Common Negotiating Pitfalls

WHETHER YOU'RE AN EXPERIENCED negotiator or are the new kid on the block, negotiating can be intimidating, confusing, and even frustrating, and you are bound to make a few mistakes along the way. That's okay; it's part of the learning process and part of the process of perfecting your negotiating technique.

Even the most experienced negotiators think about how they could have done things differently. Like chess, negotiating involves learning the rules, studying different players' styles, and developing your own skill over time. In split-second negotiating, some of these skill developments will happen, and need to happen, pretty quickly. Your ability to adapt your negotiating style, strategy, and tactics to the situation at hand, and to the negotiating medium, is extremely important.

In the past few chapters we've covered some of the common strategies, styles, and ploys used in negotiations and offered some quick defensive tactics to use when you encounter them. To help you learn and develop your negotiating style and process, this chapter offers some of the larger and more common pitfalls you need to manage or avoid altogether.

Dealing with Difficult People

Everyone has a different outlook on life. Our individual experiences influence how we see the rest of world and how we react to what we encounter. When two or more parties sit down at the negotiating table, literally or virtually, each person has a different perspective on the situation and operates from that viewpoint.

The trick is to find a way to balance all the different personalities involved in the discussion so the focus remains on the subject matter and not on the individuals themselves. Meeting this challenge can be mentally exhausting and physically tiresome if one of the personalities is uncooperative by nature or if it clashes with your own.

When the person becomes the problem, the deal-making process can be grueling and unpleasant. It's hard to concentrate on your strategy when you feel as if you're walking on eggshells, worrying about how the other person will respond to your next statement or feeling frustrated because you can't find a way to get along. Generally the way to deal with this problem is to deal with it early on by acknowledging that you do in fact have a common interest: the goals and objectives that brought you both to the table in the first place.

▶ Reaching an Understanding

If the other party refuses to be accommodating, fights you every step of the way, and continues to employ a positional negotiating style, you should examine her behavior by openly discussing it. You can try letting her know how you view the situation and talk about how your personality differences prevent the two of you from working toward a win-win outcome.

For example, you might be frustrated with her quick, defensive reactions to your requests, while she might be impatient with your slow responses. By calling attention to these differences, you might discover that she's used to working in a fast-paced environment and handling every situation with speed. She in turn could benefit from learning that your slower approach isn't meant to be obstructive; you have a tendency to analyze things. Once this is out on the table, you can work on meeting each other's personal needs, in the interest of moving forward more effectively with the negotiation.

Respect Your Opponent's Opinions

If the other party continues to be difficult, explain how you have tried to put your differences aside to create a more comfortable atmosphere. Ask that she afford you the same courtesy. Let her know that while you respect her opinions, you'd like to focus on solutions that make the deal work, not the actions that destroy its progress.

It's worth trying to understand where the other party is coming from—is there particular time or task pressure or background you should know about? It also helps to be open about where you stand and what your needs are. Don't place blame or get upset—that can make your opponent less likely to work out the problem with you. Many times when you sense anger or aggression from another party in a negotiation, that emotion has nothing to do with you or the problem at hand; it's a reflection of something else in his personal or professional life. Getting it out in the open can help both of you in your effort to arrive at a win-win conclusion.

Choose Words Carefully

The English language contains a few seemingly innocent words that can surprise you with how much power they hold. Tucked inside a harmless sentence, these words can create a tone that sounds offensive to anyone who already has a defensive personality. Although your intention is not to be hurtful, the other party misunderstands your statement and reacts negatively to it.

You can fine-tune your speech with the following word choices to avoid sounding too aggressive:

- *"I" versus "you"*—Instead of saying, "You still didn't answer my question," rephrase the statement: "I'm sorry, I still don't understand. I think a few examples can give me a better idea." By placing the blame on yourself, you make clear to the other party that you're not criticizing and she will be more willing to communicate.
- *Negative vs. positive*—Words such as can't, won't, shouldn't, and don't should be used sparingly. Instead of saying, "I can't do that" try, "I have a few other options I'd like to get your opinion on." It might be easier for you to explain why you can't accept his offer if you present alternative solutions.
- *"But"*—Think of this word as a cutoff point, beyond which your counterpart will stop listening to what you're saying. He presents his idea, you rephrase it, and immediately you follow up with a "but" statement. For example, "Our production costs are high, but the materials you're requesting are expensive." To the person on the defense, this could sound like you're attacking his original idea by telling him he's wrong to have had it in the first place. Simply remove "but" from the sentence to assure he hears your response: "Production costs are high; the supplier charges X-amount for these materials."

Whenever possible, use facts to back up your objections to the other party's request. Providing evidence for your protest helps him better understand your position and shows him you're not trying to be difficult.

▶ **Responding to Stonewalling**

Sometimes a difficult person is just that—a difficult personality or a person who uses a tough or challenging negotiating style. Sometimes a perfectly normal person with an accommodating or collaborative personality can become difficult to work with; this may reflect a genuine difficulty in his life, or he may just be stonewalling. There's a difference: stonewalling is a ploy that is purposely used to draw your attention away from the subject you're discussing, while in the other case a challenging approach may be an innate part of a person's character. To see if the other party is using the tactic, you might tell him you don't believe he's serious about negotiating with you because he's rejected every offer you've made. Go over your proposals and highlight the points that illustrate how he benefits from them. Then ask him to explain his opposition.

Letting Stress Take Over

Think about the last time you were stressed out, particularly in a negotiation. Did your face get red and your palms begin to sweat? Did your heart start to pound rapidly and your body start to shake? Did you get a headache, stomachache, or a nauseous feeling? Now think about what you were doing. Were you shouting or being shouted at? Were you emotional or crying? Did you walk out of the room and slam the door? Were you able to think rationally or perform specific duties successfully? Would you have felt comfortable making important decisions during this period of stress?

If you tend to get overly stressed in this kind of situation, particularly during a negotiation, what follows may help.

Avoid Stress

Stress, like drugs and alcohol, delivers a rush to your brain that affects your body, mind, and spirit that reduces your power to control emotions and actions, and your ability to think logically.

Unlike substance abuse, stress can be controlled as soon as it appears if you take the time to learn about how it manifests in your world. Once this is done, you can guard against your instinctive, counterproductive reactions and respond with a more constructive approach.

Know What Sets You Off

Unforgiving negotiators can try to throw you off course by tampering with your inner strengths and exposing your weaknesses. In other words, they find the buttons to push to upset you. Your first line of defense against this tactic is to know your hot buttons, and to see it coming:

- Do you get defensive when your ideas are shot down?
- Do you take it personally when you're verbally attacked?
- Do you get insulted when someone doesn't agree with you?
- Do you get angry when someone rolls his eyes at you?
- Are you easily offended? How so?
- Are you easily intimidated? What are you afraid of?
- How strongly does guilt affect you? Are you quick to give in?

Next, think about how you feel when you're put in these situations. What emotions do you feel the most? What is your body telling you?

You should try to develop your own system for dealing with stress. Go into a quiet room alone and close your eyes for, say, five minutes to regain strength. Take a few deep breaths. Take a walk around the block to expend any negative energy. Jot down your favorite quote, a passage from your favorite book, or a saying from your favorite philosopher—anything that helps you feel centered—and read it to yourself when you're feeling overwhelmed. Call or text a colleague or friend or family member. If it's music that relaxes you, take a few minutes to listen to your favorite tune.

▶ Look Both Ways Before Crossing

Not only is this sound advice when crossing a road, it comes in handy when determining whether you're about to traverse the other party's boundaries and cause even greater irritation. It's important to think before reacting. Otherwise, you could destroy the relationship by causing more stress, or feel defeated by surrendering to it—either way you lose ground in the negotiation.

If you retaliate with anger, the other party knows she has you right where she wants you: on her territory. Her hardball tactics succeeded in putting you on the defensive, and now she can use it against you every step of the way. Suddenly, she accuses you of being hard to work with, temperamental, and stubborn. Clearly, this response gets you nowhere and only succeeds in damaging the relationship.

Avoid the Easy Way Out

If your response to stressful situations is to take the easy way out and just give in, you're doing yourself a major disservice. Not only do you show the other party how weak you are, but you leave the deal feeling disappointed in yourself because you didn't hold your own. Furthermore, your counterpart will be more than happy to share with his peers his success story of how he got the best of you, a reputation you don't want to acquire.

Mishandling Concessions

Another common pitfall to guard against is the management (or mismanagement) of concessions. In Chapter 2 we discussed when you should make them and when you should ask for them. Here, we'll look at the mistakes that may cause your concessions to fall short and those that result in your giving up too much. Keep track of the concessions you give and receive; you never know when the tally can be used to influence a decision.

▶ Ask Away

When you sit down to prepare your proposal, you should do some open-ended thinking about all possible concessions. From small requests to major ones, write them all down as if you can't live without a single one (yes, even if you can!), and highlight the major ones so that you'll remember them when the discussion starts getting more intense.

Evaluate Concessions and the Competition

With today's real-time access to information, it's easier than ever to evaluate alternative concessions. Of course, you have access to your own company's product offerings, shipping charges, and so forth. But you also have access to competitive products and services at the click of a mouse. Part of the preparation process is leveraging these tools to arrive at the best set of concessions, and to know the price, cost, and value of each.

There's no need to feel greedy or afraid to ask for something you think the other party views as trivial. The truth is, you never know what your counterpart will be willing to agree to. You'll regret it later if with hindsight you realize that the concessions you didn't ask for were things you could have easily obtained. Aim high even if you think you're aiming too high; your goals might not always be as ambitious as you perceive them to be.

▶ Handing It Over

When it's your turn to make concessions, one of the biggest mistakes you may make is thinking that the other party values what you're offering as much (or as little) as you do. If your strategy is to offer something you think he wants in exchange for something you really want, the danger lies in the assumption that he will view the trade as being equal. If you take this chance and discover that he doesn't think the deal is fair, he may feel like you're trying to take advantage of him and, as a result, begin withholding concessions.

Offers Must Be Fair

Avoid making the mistake of offering something small for something big (or vice versa) by learning your counterpart's objectives ahead of time. This is especially important when your request would allow you to take a big step closer to reaching your ultimate goal. You've got to do extensive and thorough research, but it will pay off. Make fair offers, and you'll get fair offers.

Remember—when making concessions always ask for something in return. Suppose you give something away without making a request for yourself because you figure you can ask for something later. For now, you'd rather move on to a point you've been eager to discuss. Then "later" comes, and the same situation happens again. If you haven't been keeping track of concessions, you'll fail to see how much you've given away compared to how much you've received. Another drawback is that you'll have to backtrack and re-evaluate the issues under discussion at the time you gave up the concession.

Ask now, not later. Always keep the discussions moving forward and toward the closing, which leads us to the next stumbling block you may encounter.

Closing Mistakes

The blunders you make during the closing stage can be a little more costly than the others we've already discussed. At closing, your negotiations are finalized; once the deal is done, there's no looking back. Before you panic, here are some tips to restore your calm.

▶ **Don't Be Afraid**

When re-examining the details of the negotiation, you might come across a miscalculation you made or an inaccuracy in one of your concessions. You may even discover a concession that you didn't mean to make. When this happens, bring it up immediately, even if you feel embarrassed. The longer you wait, the more the other side will get comfortable with it, believing that it is permanent. Worse, it will seem as if you purposely planted the error as part of a ploy.

In addition to having the courage to point out your own mistakes, you'll need to have the courage to stand up to the other party's last-minute tactics. It's never too late to make changes, even at this stage, but you want to minimize them because it's time to get the other party to make commitments. If she asks for an extra concession here and an extra one there, don't give in just to be the good guy and help close the deal faster. Don't worry about being liked during this stage. More importantly, don't be afraid to say "no."

▶ There's Still Time

Making decisions because you feel pressured to do so is one of the worst mistakes you can make, particularly during the closing. Take all the time you need to put the final stamp on the agreements you made, and you'll feel more confident about your decisions later. Some opponents will try to pressure you deliberately, to get you to stop looking for concessions, or simply because they only have so much time to allot per negotiation—think, car salespeople.

While this slower pace may incur the wrath of your counterpart, don't be coerced into finalizing anything you're not ready for. Additionally, realize that most deadlines can be negotiated. Even if the extension is just for a few hours, use the extra time efficiently.

Risk Management for Negotiators

The use of any negotiation strategy or tactic, whether used during the body of the negotiation or at closing, carries certain risks, and naturally, it's important to determine whether those risks are worth taking.

The Challenge of Risk-Taking

Risks can be personal or professional, private or social, financial or emotional, and they're all measured differently from one person to the next. For example, you might be the kind of person who doesn't feel apprehensive about investing in stocks, but you'd never chance rejection by asking your neighbor out on a date. Before you sit down for any serious negotiation, evaluate your own tolerance for risk and ask yourself in what areas you're most comfortable with it. Negotiator, know thyself! is good advice.

One good rule of thumb when approaching risk, one that works well especially for investors: invest only what you can afford to lose. That model expands well beyond investing—any tactic or concession or offer should be measured against what you can afford to lose. And that loss can be in the short term, concerning the negotiation at hand, or longer term.

One risk you should never feel good about taking is skipping the preparation stage. Your strength comes from knowledge. If you know what you're talking about, you'll feel like you're competent enough to get positive results. You'll also be less likely to back down, which puts not only your self-esteem at risk but also the other party's respect for you.

Keeping Objectives in Focus

Losing focus on objectives is a common—and dangerous—pitfall in negotiation. You get so caught up in the moment or with the minutiae or personal dynamics of the situation that the original objectives can fade into background. The danger, of course, is that you don't accomplish what you set out to accomplish in the first place—or worse, give away the store.

You really can't go wrong if you always have a clear view of your main goals. The emotions of anger, anxiety, or feeling overwhelmed can be distracting, but if you keep track of your main goals, not only are you more likely to avoid the negative effects of these distractions; you're less likely to experience the emotions in the first place.

Remaining goal oriented also involves memorizing the other party's goals in addition to keeping your own in the forefront. This knowledge gives you leverage and helps you counter the other party's tactics when the time comes. It also reminds the other party, time and time again, that you're working toward solutions that satisfy both your agendas. Bottom line: always keep an eye on the big picture.

Case Study:
When You're Feeling Underexposed

As President, CEO, and CPO of RGB Photographic, you have been toiling away at the negotiation for two hours. You've been showing your best pictures, explaining your best packages, and still, your opponents at Trindle glaze over. You don't think you're connecting. In fact, the Trindle executives seem even a bit perturbed and irritated—they have buildings to build, after all, and other things to do.

What do you do?

Rule number one is "Don't give up." You can still get the deal, especially if you feel you have the best product or service. It probably makes sense to ask for a break, so you and your opponent can collect your wits. But don't—don't—let this break actually end the negotiation. Tease the Trindle folks with a few tidbits that you might have to offer at the end of the break. Maybe you have some more cool photos to show them or better yet, a finished and printed album of work that just may catch their eye (and a good thing, in your prep work, that you saved your ace in the hole for something like this.)

During the break, if you feel antagonism or friction from one individual, try to neighbor with that individual. Find out if the irritant is related to process or product—that is, is he uncomfortable with the negotiation process and how it is unfolding, or is he uncomfortable with what you have to offer and the cost? A little informal research can yield some key info, as well as soothe the nerves of both this adversary and yourself.

The best thing is to take the break and come back with something short, sweet, compelling, and that directly addresses Trindle's needs if you can figure that out. Even throw in some favorite art photos if you think it will break the tension. Since you're operating in real time, during the break you can go to your website or blog and spin this up pretty quickly.

After some time you reconvene. Everyone's feeling a bit better. They've had a chance to check their e-mail and make sure Trindle hasn't fallen apart in their absence. They've refreshed themselves and stretched their legs with a quick stroll outside in the summer sunshine. And you've had a chance to do some research. You've discovered that in the past one of the most successful initiatives Trindle took was in the form of a series of contests in which clients who signed leases early were entered in a sweepstakes drawing for an all-expenses-paid trip to the Caribbean. The contest generated considerable publicity and led to an upswing in Trindle's leasing rates.

You take a deep breath and propose a new idea—one that hasn't been on the table before. RGB Photographic will sponsor a contest in which the winner will get a free helicopter ride during one of your photo shoots. You'll take care of all the details, arrange the helicopter ride, and so on. But Trindle will get the publicity from it.

There's silence as everyone absorbs this new idea, and then discussion breaks out as you all begin to work out its implications.

Split-Second Takeaways

1. Balance the personalities involved in any negotiation.

2. Choose your words carefully.

3. Learn your risk tolerance and study that of your opponent.

4. Keep your objectives in focus throughout the negotiation.

Chapter 8
High-Pressure Negotiating Tactics

AS WE'VE TOUCHED ON in earlier chapters, negotiators can use numerous tactics and ploys to divert your attention away from the main issues. Among these may be an assortment of high-pressure tactics that force you to make hurried decisions out of fear of losing the deal altogether. These maneuvers can take the form of competitive offers, real and imaginary deadlines, and ultimatums, all of which apparently leave little room for further negotiation.

In today's split-second negotiations, the drive to reach a conclusion may seem more pressing than ever. Everything happens fast. Everyone has to take another call or respond to another IM or move on to the next big thing. It's important to discern true pressuring tactics from those meant to simply cut to the chase and save time.

Once you learn how to recognize and counter these tactics, you'll discover that you have more negotiating room than you think.

Unrealistic First Offer

Making an unrealistic first offer is one way to get a "feel" for how much (or how little) the other party is willing to give you. You can use the other party's reaction to the offer. First, based on his expression— anger, dissatisfaction, surprise, composure, or eagerness—you can get an idea about what is either acceptable to him or within the scope of what he's willing to negotiate. Second, the more unrealistic your first offer, the more room you have to negotiate to the offer you're really willing to settle on.

▶ **Offending the Other Party**

Sometimes the other party takes offense to this kind of tactic, especially if she is well prepared and has researched the market to come up with her own number. If her knowledge is extensive in the subject or if she has several alternatives, don't start off too far off the mark. She'll be aware of what you're doing and it might backfire.

Is He Being Sincere?

Before you draw conclusions about the other party's reaction to your unrealistic offer, determine whether the emotions he displays are sincere. Ask why he's reacting the way he is. Are his reactions the result of your offer being too low? Or is he employing distracting tactics to see if he can boost it?

The other party's surprised reaction to your offer might also be an indication of whether she has a back-up plan. Her strong response could be an attempt to get a better offer than the one she already has (or thinks she can get) from someone else.

▶ **Preventative Measures**

You can avoid getting an unrealistic offer from the other party by making sure that you are the one who makes the first offer. This strategy will also enable you to secure the starting point from which you'll be negotiating—to gain the high ground, so to speak. If the other party beats you to it, however, remember to keep your cool. Although you might be quite satisfied with the offer, be careful not to show your satisfaction. She might realize her mistake and try to make up for it later when you're discussing a different issue.

Another way to counter the other party's unrealistic offer is to ignore it completely. Start talking about something else to tactfully deliver the message that you're not happy with the offer.

If you do intend to make the first offer, be careful not to put yourself at a disadvantage. If you're not sure of the rules of the game, you may err on the side of caution. Your offer might be less to your advantage than the one the other party had intended to make.

"One Time Only" Offer

Remember all that time and effort you put into preparing yourself for this negotiation? Well, don't let it all go to waste by succumbing to a phony take-it-or-leave-it tactic that turns your hard work into something done in vain. This is a common ploy meant to make you feel an enormous amount of pressure to close the deal quickly.

Decide When You're Ready to Decide

Never, never, never make a decision you're not ready to make, especially when the other party makes you feel like you're under the gun. Have you ever forgotten the one thing you were supposed to take with you to the office because you were so late and were literally running out the door? That's how you'll feel at the end of a negotiating session in which you've made a decision not based on the merits of the offer but on its time frame.

Split-second negotiating does not mean making ill-informed, hasty decisions. It means adapting your research and decision-making process to the new demands of today's information-based economy.

Most of us simply do not perform at our best in high-pressure situations; there isn't enough time to think things through. When a negotiator approaches you with a "one time only" offer, he's trying to catch you off guard and may be bluffing.

In the old days, by telling you that you had two hours to make a decision, he was not giving you the appropriate amount of time to do additional research, consult your team, or weigh the pros and cons of the situation. You were also not given the chance to ask important questions or reassess your goals and objectives. In today's split-second world, that time has shortened considerably, and with it the time in which you'll be asked to make a decision. Now, instead of two hours, your colleague may ask for an answer in two minutes.

Get Organized

Nowadays, with Internet connectivity and fast communication tools, you may be able to sort through a one-time two-hour offer pretty effectively, but you must be organized and prepared to do this.

▶ **Ignore the Tactic**

When the other party introduces the "one time offer" into the discussion, ignore it. Continue talking about the ongoing issues or bring up some new ones. Remember, he may only be trying to intimidate or bluff you. See if he brings it up again before you respond.

▶ **The Real Deal**

On rare occasions when the other party really is in a crunch for time (and to find out if this is the case, ask for specific details of why the deal has to be done fast), try to get an extension on the deadline. Whether it's for an extra day or for an extra week, any additional length of time will give you the opportunity to weigh your alternatives and re-examine your goals to see if they're being met.

Delay of Game

Delaying the game is the opposite of the deadline ploy. Delay tactics are used by negotiators in a variety of ways: to stall, to test your urgency, or to temporarily appease you. It's okay to give the other party some time to absorb everything so he feels comfortable about the decisions he's about to make, but set a limit. Don't let him take advantage of you.

Delay as a Tactic

Some negotiators purposely ask for a delay so they can mull everything over before making the commitment. They should tell you up front how much time they need. If you've traveled quite a distance to meet with them, two to three hours should be sufficient, especially in today's interconnected world.

► Stalling Negotiations

Stalling occurs when a negotiation is brought to a halt. By digging her heels in, the other party decides she simply cannot go any further because your requests are unacceptable. Naturally, you'll begin to think about what concessions you can offer in order to keep the negotiation moving forward. However, before making concessions, ask her point blank what she would consider to be acceptable. Find out exactly what the obstructing element is, and try to work the issue out before you give her anything more.

► Testing Urgency

You'll want to be careful about how you react to the other party's delay because there may be only one reason he's using it: to see how desperate you are for his business. It may seem like a silly cat-and-mouse game, but sometimes you have no choice but to play along. When you do, it'll go something like this. The other party calls for a delay, you agree, then nothing happens. No phone calls. No e-mails. No contact of any kind. If you initiate contact, say the next day, the other party will know that you have no alternatives, that he has the upper hand, and that he can get more concessions out of you.

As tough as it might be, you really need to wait this one out and let him come to you. Even more difficult is determining how long you should wait for a response. While you don't want to seem eager, you don't want to let too many days slip by without hearing a word. Motivate him to give you a decision by giving him a deadline; tell him all deals are off the table if you don't have his answer by a specified time.

▶ The Check Is in the Mail

We've all heard that one before! This six-word phrase was designed to give the person on the receiving end a false sense of security. A negotiator uses this tactical delay not to pressure you but to take the pressure off him and buy more time to fulfill his obligation.

Sometimes the system is slow, and there's nothing anybody can do about it. If you've experienced this over and over with the same company, let them know you're not a pushover by finding something to take away from them (the report you promised, the early shipment you said you'd arrange) until they deliver.

The Other Option Option

Remember to use your backup plan as leverage. Tell the other party you have another option that you plan to pursue if he can't reach a decision. Don't be aggressive, but do make him aware that you're giving him the first opportunity and you have to have a commitment from him soon. Make clear to him that he's not your only option in this matter.

The Bottom Line

Some negotiators love to use a bogus bottom line, or ultimatum—a point beyond which the deal is not negotiable. For example, the person you're negotiating with might say that her supervisor will not allow her to decrease the price lower than a certain number. Giving a false bottom line is a way to avoid having to negotiate many concessions, and it can be used in just about any situation.

The way to face this tactic is to call attention away from the bottom-line number by focusing on the topics that interest your opponent the most. Whenever the other party zeroes in on one particular issue—in this case, price—get her to stop looking at problems with tunnel vision and start examining the negotiation as a whole—service, delivery, warranty—other elements that make a deal a deal. Resist strongly the idea that any negotiation is *only* about one thing; there are always other parts in a negotiation that can become bargaining points.

False Concessions

Let's say you walk into a store to look at the gorgeous jacket you saw in the window. A salesperson approaches you and says, "The jacket costs $75, but for you, I'll sell it for $65." She wants to let you know up front that she's giving you the deal of the century on this thing. You smile politely and go back to the jacket to look over the pockets and buttons, when suddenly she says, "Okay, it seems you really like this jacket so I'll give it to you for $55." Another discount? Now you're really interested! You inquire about the fiber content, wash instructions, and so on, and the salesperson reduces the price another $10. Feeling like you just hit the jackpot, you pay for the jacket and leave a satisfied customer. Five minutes later another prospective customer walks into the store and starts looking at the jacket, wherein the keen salesperson says, "The jacket costs $85, but for you, I'll sell it for $75."

In both instances, the seller had a set figure in her mind the whole time. By exaggerating the price and then handing out a few concessions, she made it seem like you got a great bargain right there on the spot.

The First Offer

Retailers often use the "exaggerated first offer" tactic in conjunction with the multiple concessions tactic to make a deal seem better.

When you encounter a situation in which a concession is made at the onset of a negotiation, there are a few things to be aware of before you make a decision. Is the seller asking for anything in return? If not, chances are that it's not a real concession. (Remember one of our first rules of negotiating: when you make a concession, always ask for something in return.) Is the dollar amount being significantly lowered or are you given a range? If the salesperson has switched to a price range, chances are she won't come down in price beyond the range offer.

Using Competition as Leverage

Here, you use real competition or competitive offerings as a type of shill in the negotiation. This tactic works extremely well when trying to decide which cell-phone carrier to subscribe to. Call several wireless companies to hear each of their offers, then go back to the one with the most attractive offer and mention that you are also looking into such-and-such company and were quoted a rate that you're seriously considering. Nine times out of ten, you'll get another offer right away. Continue doing this until the best deal presents itself.

Now suppose the roles reverse, and your opponent is the one with several other options. He is out looking for the best offer, and he won't hesitate to let you know it. Be careful. You don't know for a fact that your competitors have made better offers, and there's a chance the opponent is bluffing. If you encounter a situation like this, get the other party to talk about what he likes about your product or what he doesn't like about your competitor's product. You'll get a better idea if the offers are real.

Deadlines—For Better or for Worse

Deadlines—either intermediate or final—can be used not only to keep a negotiation on track but also to put pressure on negotiators. Especially with today's split-second negotiations, deadlines may be in a day, in a few hours, or even in a few minutes. The pace of today's business almost always brings a deadline into play somewhere along the line.

▶ Deadlines as a High Pressure Tool

Deadlines may be mutually agreed upon or may be set by one of the negotiating teams. While the opposing negotiator may not say so explicitly, the intent is often to cash in by asking for last-minute concessions. Typically (and this is what the other party is betting on), we're more apt to compromise when we're experiencing time restraints. When too much is coming at us all at once, it's easier to get rid of the most immediate, stressful factor, and then take the time to work it out.

▶ Make Sure the Deadline Is Real

Deadlines, especially unilateral deadlines set by one party, may be real or may be arbitrary as part of a tactic to put a rush on a deal. If the deadline is uncomfortably tight, it's worth probing the origin of the deadline with questions. It's probably worth asking up front how much flexibility there is in the deadline. The answers can give an idea whether the deadline is real, and can also indicate whether the deadline itself is a negotiating point.

Some deadlines may be more informal or made out of convenience than others. "I have to catch a flight at 3 o'clock this afternoon" indicates a deadline, but perhaps not an insurmountable one as a later flight may be available or the discussion can continue via e-mail. Again, a few questions—and a willingness to offer a concession or benefit to the opponent for staying longer—might help.

Get Charged Up!

Today's technological world can create a lot more "deadlines" in any negotiation or discussion. The life of a principal negotiator's cell phone or laptop battery can make a lot of difference. If you're running a negotiation it might be a good idea to advise everyone to "charge up" before the meeting or avoid the use of battery-powered devices altogether. To have a negotiation break down because a principal negotiator or "fact guy" runs out of juice should be avoided.

▶ **Last-Minute Offers**

The last-minute offer is another method the other party uses to try to sway your decision. For example, if the lease is almost up on your apartment, the landlord will wait until the end of the month to inform you of the rate increase because he assumes you haven't decided to move out and will need to extend the lease. Similarly, you might hold out on informing the landlord of your decision to stay because you assume no one else is interested in the apartment; after all, you haven't indicated you're leaving.

Although most leases have a thirty-day notice written into their contracts, this example illustrates how important leverage is. If you wait until the last minute to keep your apartment, you can almost guarantee the landlord has three interested parties lined up, all willing to accept a higher price.

Quick Settlements

Tight deadlines can lead to quick settlements, and the team with the most effective "quick settlement" approach can win. Effective quick settlements are often a function of being informed and being organized, which in turn allow you to research and present things quickly and effectively. You and your negotiating team should pre-research possible items to include in the negotiation, and may even want to role play or rehearse the delivery of quick settlement options. Quick settlements can bring relief to both sides when tight deadlines are involved, and are likely to lead to a greater win for the side that leads in making the settlement. Particularly in today's split-second negotiating era, the ability to make a quick settlement is an important asset.

▶ **Withholding Information**

Sometimes the other party will wait until the deadline is near to disclose additional information, leaving you little time to digest the new details. She wants to see how far you'll bend, hoping that you're too frazzled to put your best foot forward. This one's hard to defend against: ask for more time if possible, or take some of your concessions off the table to restore equilibrium. But remember: you may have to react *quickly*—far more swiftly than you were used to in the past. That's just the nature of today's business.

▶ Setting Deadlines on the Fly

There are many ways to use deadlines in your favor. One of the most discouraging aspects of a negotiation is feeling as if you're getting nowhere. If the other party is stalling and you're ready to move on, return to the focus of the discussion by instituting a deadline that causes her to spring back into action. Make it apparent that she's in danger of losing your business if she doesn't give you a decision by a specified time and date, at which point all deals will be off. Remember, work toward both your and the other party's goals, but don't allow her to push you around.

If two of your other alternatives have already made you offers, take advantage of setting a deadline that urges the party you're dealing with now to make an offer before the others expire and you're no longer able to compare all three. Be considerate when presenting the limitation so as not to offend the other person, and just give her the facts: "I hope I can have your offer today because I'm expecting two others this evening."

You Need Deadlines

There's no easy way to deliver a deadline without causing the other party to be a little miffed. No matter how gently you approach the subject, she's going to get upset because you're putting her in a difficult position. Using tact and matter-of-factness will help.

▶ Removing Deadlines on the Fly

If you sense that, after a deadlock, things are going okay, or if you're getting the concessions you seek, it may help to extend the deadline. You're on a roll. Depending on the situation, it may be better to keep the original tight deadline, for this is the source of your success in the first place. Any time you can get what you want *without* pressuring the other team, you will build a better relationship for the future.

▶ Waiting It Out

Most concessions are made toward the end of a negotiation's deadline, if there is one. The explanation is simple. The more time the two parties invest in the negotiation process, the less likely they will be to pull out. If one party begins demanding new concessions, the opponents are more likely to give in so that negotiations can come to a successful end. However, sitting tight until the end and then asking for additional concessions is a high-risk strategy, and you will need patience and self-confidence to use it.

Your counterpart is aware of this strategy, and it is quite likely he'll try to use it. When he does, counter the tactic by examining his position:

- What is his motivation?
- Is he trying to buy time, and if so, why?
- What does he hope to achieve?
- What does he stand to lose?
- If you opt out, how does that affect his plan?
- Does he have a hidden agenda?

Another way to use patience as a tactic—one that's not so chancy—is to acquire more time to conduct additional research. If you have drawn a number of conclusions about your counterpart or speculated why the company he works for is putting pressure on him to close the deal, it's in your best interest to dig a little deeper to test your assumptions. You might be surprised to discover just how important your deal is to them.

When the eleventh hour rolls around, don't be opposed to extending the negotiation if it means the best deal can be worked out if given more time. The best win-win may come this way.

Case Study:
Does the Competitor Have a Longer Lens?

Despite your offer to sponsor a contest, Trindle continues to drag its feet, and the negotiating session stretches out. It seems that every time you try to move toward settlement of a point, the Trindle executives want to move to something else. Right now they've focused on your competition.

As the President/CEO/CPO of RGB Photographic, you're used to hearing this one a lot: "Yes, that's a nice offer, but your competition CMY Photographic offers us services X and Y for $Z less than you do."

Okay, is it for real, or is Trindle using it as a negotiation ploy? You'd just jump out of your skin to know.

The first thing to do (that is, if you haven't prepped yourself with your competition's offerings already by looking at their sites and in particular, talking to some of their clients) is to go online while the Trindle executives are talking. See if CMY even does the kind of work you're doing. Then one of your first replies might be, "You know, CMY Photographic mainly does weddings. Shooting a bride and her party is a fine art, but it hardly compares to the lighting work, size, and scale of what I do. And I'm not even sure the guy from CMY has ever been in a helicopter!"

You should be armed—and prepared—for any ploys involving competitors or supposed competitive offers. The more you can know about the competition beforehand, of course, the better. And sometimes dealing with the competitive ploy is just plain common sense.

One of the Trindle people brings up another point, and you're ready for him. "So you're telling me that you might have someone come in from New York to do these shots? That's great, and you might be able to get more consistent photos around the country if you do that. But these guys better be pretty good meteorologists, for I'd hate to see them fly out only to find that it's cloudy all day and they can't get up for that aerial. Are you sure you want to do it that way?"

Bargaining under pressure often means taking what's thrown at you, and throwing it back with something better, or something your client never thought of.

Split-Second Takeaways

1. Study high-pressure techniques in order to counter them.

2. Don't make a deal you don't want to make.

3. Don't be pressured by false deadlines.

Chapter 9
When to Close, and When to Walk Away

THE ANALOGY MIGHT BE trite, but the phases of the negotiation process may resemble a dating relationship. There's a period of discovery, a period of give-and-take, and a resolution. Like a dating sequence, at some point you and your partner (or you *or* your partner) will be ready, deadline or not, to bring the thing to a close and to finalize a deal. That deal might drop straight out of a period of harmonious discussion, or it might be that after hours, days, or weeks of negotiating, you're still pretty far apart and not ready to "tie the knot" just yet. This chapter is about deciding what to do at these late "resolution" stages of the negotiating process.

Solving Unequal Bargaining Problems

If the negotiation has been smooth up to this point, the terms and concessions should be fairly easy to document and to spin up into a deal. If there's time, the negotiating team can document all elements of the deal on the spot, draw up the final agreement and get the necessary signatures, real or virtual, right now.

Formulating the agreement can be formal, or it can be a matter of taking notes and distributing to the parties later for final review and ratification. Sometimes it helps to give the resolution some time to sit in everyone's mind before finalizing it, perhaps in another meeting or conference. If you feel the negotiations have gone in your favor more than the other side's, you may want to avoid this "cooling off" period and proceed with the final deal right then and there.

If the negotiation hasn't arrived at an equal, win-win deal, there's more work to do. Various tactics can be employed to resolve one-sided deals, and if they can't be resolved, setting the negotiation aside for now may be the best option.

One Winner, One Loser

A win-lose outcome results when positional negotiating tactics dominate the majority of the bargaining process. In such a situation one person strives to get the better deal over the other. This comes about because both parties have their feet firmly planted on their side of the fence, neither willing to move. They act irrationally toward each other, using pride and arrogance to focus on their ultimate goal of satisfying the ego instead of focusing on a positive solution for both parties.

This behavior can be destructive to business dealings because the results, especially long term, may be negative for both companies even if they're temporarily positive for the "winning" negotiator. Because the negotiator, or negotiators, focused on maintaining their positions, they could not establish trust or communicate their goals and objectives. When winning becomes more important than finding the best solution, both parties will suffer. Frustration more than anything else will serve as the catalyst for making and agreeing to concessions, in which the competition becomes a game of "The more I get, the less I have to give."

When No One Wins

A deadlock occurs when negotiations come to an impasse, in which both parties have used up all their concessions. Progress seems out of reach, and no matter how many times you go over the issues, favorable solutions are nowhere in sight. Both parties lose because neither side accomplished their goals. Additionally, the emotional response to such a stalemate can bring anger and blame, potentially, and a communication collapse. Both parties withdraw from the discussion tactically and emotionally, and in some cases, want to save face and not "budge" back into the negotiation. It's a lose-lose situation.

Getting Things Going Again

Although it may seem so at the time, no deadlock is permanent. Time, positive attitude, and an open mind can get even the most deadlocked negotiations going again.

Deadlock often occurs because the best possible solution hasn't been discovered yet. If the other party seems inflexible, there may be something being held out of the discussion that could breathe new life into it. The opponent may or may not be aware of this element, so it's up to you to try to get it out of her. You might want to reconvene the meeting and do some brainstorming and creative thinking to get these alternative ideas onto the table.

A short or even a lengthy break may help. When you reconvene, a review of objectives and some smaller points of agreement might help. Sometimes it's better to focus on what you *have* accomplished than what you haven't—It gets the positive energy back into the room and makes both parties realize they can agree on *something*.

Knowing When to Opt Out

Sometimes, no matter how much time you've invested into making a deal work, there comes a point where you feel it's time to walk away. The reasons might be readily apparent—you're not satisfied with the final offer, you have new information, you're uncomfortable with the other party and its tactics, one (or more) of your alternatives presented a better offer, or you want to do more research and seek a better alternative.

Other reasons are more psychological or intuitive. For example, if your counterpart has been quarrelsome, demanding, rude, and difficult to work with from the very beginning, you'll wonder if you want to deal with this person through the life of the contract, as the behavior may not improve. You should also think about whether you'd want a long-term relationship and have to negotiate with him *again* for another deal.

Opting out can just as often be a matter of instinct as of facts or concrete evidence. When you don't feel like the other party is holding up his end of the deal or looking for the win-win, withdrawing from the negotiation not only saves you time, stress, and sometimes money, but it also sends a message to the other party that you're too far apart, factually or emotionally, to continue. Most likely, if there is a win-win somewhere in sight, he will come back to the table. If he doesn't, the best course may be to assume that it wouldn't have worked anyway. You can then move forward to another negotiation with someone else.

Clinching the Deal

You're almost there! Exciting as that may sound, you still have a few more challenges to overcome. These trials will no doubt test your perseverance, determination, and skill, but they will also bring you closer to reaching a well-deserved closure and help you avoid roadblocks that can (and often do) prevent this agreement from happening.

Knowing What to Expect

When you're in the thick of a negotiation, it's easy to get caught up swapping concessions and making offers and counteroffers. You're trying to keep up with deciphering the other person's body language, mood, sincerity, and next move. You must constantly take stock of how much leverage you have, re-evaluate where you stand with your give-and-takes, and reaffirm that your goals are being met. You may well meet the end with a sigh of relief.

Last-Minute Bargaining

People have a tendency to panic when time is almost up, partly out of fear of losing your business, partly out of fear they won't achieve their goals. As a result, deals of all sorts may come out of the woodwork in a desperate attempt to keep the negotiation moving. This can benefit you if the other side gets caught up in it, but be careful not to give away the store on your side.

You can expect a lot to happen during the final stages of the negotiation. Here are a few more helpful tips:

▶ Separate Closure from the Rest

Closing comes with its own set of obstacles you'll need to get around and involves thought, and sometimes, creativity. Regard it as a review of everything you and the other party have discussed. Some agreements could have been made so long ago (hours, days, months), they'll need to be reiterated and verified.

When you're ready to close, ask your counterpart if he agrees that it's time to close. If so, clearly state that everything you'll be discussing from here on out will be part of the closure. A time for closing discussion can be set in advance in the agenda or simply agreed to along the way. If your opponent isn't sure he is ready, give him some time if he requests it.

▶ Working Through Objections

Since closure requires the go-ahead from both parties, problems could arise if one party objects to one or more of the terms. In this case, you'll have to use your best negotiating skills, and probably a degree of patience, to work through the objections and preclude deadlock. You're close to the end—the last thing you want to do is jeopardize the relationship and hinder clear decision-making. Acknowledge that the disagreements are sound, even if you don't think they are; your counterpart is more likely to treat you with the same courtesy. Work with the other party, not against her, to pinpoint where the problems lie.

Bring Out the Objection Underneath

If you sense there's a deeper issue than your counterpart is willing to admit, ask some exploratory questions to coax it out, like, "It seems like you're feeling something's not quite right—is there another issue that concerns you?" Be empathetic, and offer to help.

Make sure every issue is dealt with right then and there. Otherwise, it becomes harder to resolve when deeper into the agreement.

When and How to Close

Though you should always be looking for opportunities to close, there are some obvious and some not-so-obvious signals telling you the moment is right to make this vital move. If all parties feel their goals and objectives have been achieved, then you're ready to move on.

At this point, you're probably eager to make it official—but hold on, there is one more thing you need to do: Allow time for you and your team, and your counterpart and his or her team, to go over the notes you made throughout the course of the discussion. This may be especially important in a split-second negotiation because everything happens so fast.

On a separate sheet of paper, outline all the agreements that were made and the details and terms that were discussed. List your concessions, the other party's concessions, concessions that were grouped together, and any contingencies that were made regarding these decisions. Write everything as clearly and thoroughly as you understand it to be. If everything goes smoothly, these will be the terms of your contract.

When Is the Deal Closed?

From a legal standpoint, closure occurs when all the agreed-upon details are finalized into a legally binding, signed contract, witnessed and verified by all parties. Read the entire contract, and sign when you're ready. Take your time and feel good about what you've accomplished!

Next, compare your notes with those of your counterpart, or if he didn't take notes, read each item on your list out loud. The point is to be sure that both you and the other party understand the agreement in the same way. If you thought he was paying the shipping charges in exchange for a 20 percent discount on production fees but he thought he was paying 20 percent of the shipping, you'll want to work that out.

▶ Last-Minute Concessions

When things aren't going as smoothly as you hoped, and the other party is still unable to accept the conditions as they stand, you might want to offer a last-minute concession. Not a big one but one that is worth something to them. This gesture shows the other person that you're willing to sacrifice something to make the deal work for both of you. If giving up a minor concession means something major to your counterpart and to the deal as a whole, go for it. Wouldn't you feel better walking away from the table together, to celebrate a mutual achievement, instead of gloating alone about a victory? Worse, derailing the whole deal? Herein lies the beauty of win-win negotiating.

What's Stopping You?

As strange as it sounds, some people never really want to reach the end of a negotiation. They might experience more anxiety at the closing stage than during the bargaining stage. The deal might represent a big step and a big commitment.

Remember that feeling you had when you bought your first car? First computer? First home? After spending months researching, comparing, and reworking your budget to make the best possible purchase, you reach that part of the transaction when you're just about ready to make your dream a reality. You're excited, nervous, pensive, happy, and unsure all at once. Furthermore, if it's a "split-second" deal, you may be concerned that not all bases have been covered and not all facts or elements are really known or understood. So how are you ever going to make it through the closing with that in mind?

▶ Overcoming Fear

Negotiating may seem intimidating at first, but once you get going, you feel more comfortable. During the negotiation process, you experience many emotions and you learn how to work through them as you resolve the issues under discussion. But when closing time nears, those old feelings seem to return to the forefront. The closing is your final step—you don't get to come back to the table tomorrow to hash out the details again. That in itself is enough to scare anyone off! If you've been prepared the entire time, covered all your major points, and feel good about how the other party fared, then you've done your job and deserve to give yourself (and your counterpart) the opportunity to close the deal, write it down, and make it official.

▶ Controlling Doubt

While questions about details such as price, discounts, and deadlines are often easily answered, intangible questions that create uncertainty and doubt can prevent you from making the commitment. You might have doubts about whether you made the best possible deal, and you may continue to fear that you've omitted something important from the conversation or from the deal.

All of these mental blocks will cause you to second-guess yourself and lose faith in a deal you felt good about closing just five minutes ago. Don't let your confidence be shattered with your own doubt. It's okay to feel apprehensive, but take control of it before it ruins what you've worked so hard to achieve.

Moreover, by dragging your feet, you run the risk of forfeiting your counterpart's respect and possibly the deal. He might lose his patience or begin to have questions of his own, and the last thing you want to do is give him time to second-guess himself too. Have faith in yourself, your work, and the negotiation, and close the deal knowing you did the best you could possibly do.

Is Fear Preventing Me from Closing the Deal?

If there's time, take a break and review everything with a colleague or friend. Review your goals and ask yourself if they've been met; seek positive reinforcement in the objectives you completed. If you feel good about the facts, your reluctance is probably borne out of fear.

Extras and Perks

If you're ready to close but the other party is still ambivalent, there are a few things you can do to help ease him into closure. In addition to helping you bring your negotiation to a successful conclusion, extras and perks can help you show a dose of good faith and character that may move the deal to conclusion.

As stated previously, you should always be trying to develop a good relationship with your counterparts, whether you're verifying information with them during the preparation stage, bargaining with them during the negotiating stage, or composing the contract together. The relationships you begin building today will over time blossom into great friendships and successful partnerships that both of you can continue to benefit from. A few extras or perks thrown in at the last minute, maybe a discount or even a sample of your company's product, a nice dinner or gift card or even just refreshments afterwards or paying for parking can win some valuable points.

▶ Be Reassuring

A little enthusiasm goes a long way, especially when the other party shows hesitation. Just a few encouraging words may be just what she needs to hear to move on. You can also point out all the objectives she's accomplished. Sometimes hearing them listed out loud makes a bigger impact than just quietly thinking them over. Go over any deadlines that were agreed on. Say something like, "By June 1, you'll have the first shipment so you'll be able to ship to your customers way ahead of schedule." This will help the other party get a clear picture of how she benefits from the transactions that took place. Positive energy is contagious, so use it often.

▶ Be Considerate

As part of your planning, compile a list of several small concessions that you wouldn't mind giving up, if needed. Use them as backup for when you need to apply a little push. Your counterpart will certainly appreciate the favor, and hopefully that will be all she needs to overcome last-minute indecision.

Avoid Renegotiating

While it's good to have something in reserve for emergencies, be careful you don't give too much away. Once you've agreed to close, leave it at that. Don't try to rehash issues you've already agreed on—you could be opening up a can of worms.

Starting with the End in Mind

The key to a successful close is thinking about it from the first moments of the negotiation process. Everything you do—researching, planning, bargaining, relationship building—should be done with the close in mind. When researching, think about what you can use as last-minute concessions; when planning, have backups set in place at every stage of the game, and come up with answers to "what if" questions; while bargaining, continue to move forward and take steps to avoid an impasse. Through the process, create a positive environment and atmosphere that would support a close. You want to satisfy your goals, and the overall goal is to get to the close and make everything official.

Integrity, Integrity, Integrity

The key to great negotiating is integrity—being able to make a commitment and to follow through on the promise. This is a big reason why you must be certain to understand all of the terms you're agreeing to. Don't kick the can down the road by making sloppy agreements—it'll come back to bite later on, and your next negotiation could turn out to be a nightmare.

Remember, closing is a separate step that requires as much diligence as the other steps. You should never rush through it. Here are the closing checkpoints you need to be sure you follow through with:

1. First, confirm that everyone is in agreement, making sure everything has been worked out and there's nothing left to close. Use the list of concessions you made to once again verify all terms and conditions, if needed.

2. Next, review the agenda to be sure everything has been covered and all major points have been discussed.

3. Finally, create a few to-do lists, recording deadlines to follow up on and deadlines to meet.

The Moment of Glory

Congratulations! The closing is finished, and it's time to sign the contracts. Grab your finest champagne glasses along with your favorite ballpoint pen and make a toast to yourself, your counterpart, and the success of your negotiation! Reward yourself for all your hard work—go out for dinner, throw a party for your colleagues, celebrate! You've certainly earned it.

Case Study: Closing the Deal

The coffee pot is cold, the plate of Danishes is empty, and the energy level in the room is winding down. You've made a strong case for your company, RGB Photographic, and Trindle and Trundle has agreed to most of your points. There are a few details to still work out, but your sense is that further discussion is going to needlessly annoy people and conceivably re-introduce issues that have already been settled.

So you take a deep breath and say, "I think we're at the point of wrapping this up. Can I just run down a brief list of what we've agreed to and what we're still discussing. Then I think we could leave these smaller points to the lawyers to work out."

This is the moment the whole process has been building toward, the point at which you come to an agreement and do the deal. So you're sure, when making the final closing, to hit on these points:

1. Refer back to your notes and say, from time to time: "As we said when we were discussing this point . . ." You even bring in the names of Trindle and Trundle executives from time to time: "You made a very good point about this issue, Ed, so we agreed . . ."

2. Establish clear agreement on which points haven't yet been settled and set a time frame for working them out: "We can ask our lawyers to meet on these points next week and have a formalized agreement by May 30. Does that sound okay?"

3. Push to write the contract. As noted above, this will give you more control over the precise wording of the terms of the agreement and places the initiative firmly with you.

As everyone stands up, you say, cheerfully, "I think this calls for a celebration. How about if RGB treats all of you to a drink at the restaurant next door and we'll celebrate our new working partnership?"

Split-Second Takeaways

1. Know when to close a deal and when to walk.

2. Use benefits/perks to close difficult deals.

3. Recognize your goal when you get to it.

Chapter 10
Under Contract

A SPLIT-SECOND NEGOTIATION MIGHT get to a fast agreement and conclusion, but the job isn't done quite yet. You need to formalize the agreement into a written deal. A contract or some other detailed form of agreement is essential to execute and manage the deal going forward. The contract doesn't have to be very elaborate—concise is usually best—but it does need to cover the main points of the discussion.

In a split-second negotiation, a final agreement or contract becomes even more important—and more difficult to do, for everything happens so fast and key points may get lost. That said, the split-second contract is more likely than not to be concise!

Although the details of a contract are normally not fleshed out until the end of a meeting, it's important to keep them in mind throughout the entire negotiation period. Good note taking will not only ensure you include everything you want in the contract, but it will also help clear up any fuzzy points discussed hours or even days beforehand.

Elements of a Contract

Contracts serve to record agreements that two or more parties have made with each other and to outline the terms of those agreements. A good contract should protect the promises, expectations, and investments of the parties involved, and if done right, is sufficient to be enforced or to resolve disputes in a court of law.

There are several different types of contracts, ranging from a template contract you find online to a specific contract written up following negotiations.

► Form Contracts

Form or boilerplate contracts are pre-crafted templates that are used for basic, often repeated agreements. Most real estate agencies and mortgage brokers will use the same form contract for every client, listing the conditions, limitations, and delivery expectations the company demands, amending the boilerplate only to reflect the terms and provisions unique to each situation. The set-in-stone appearance of this type of contract may seem intimidating. But it is possible to change the form, to add or "line out" something as needed, so long as both parties agree. Both parties should initial the changes.

The Parts of a Contract

At its roots, a contract has three parts: the offer, the acceptance, and consideration. The offer is straightforward: "We at Company A will produce 1,000 widgets per month for the next 6 months." The consideration is the payment: "Company B will pay $25 per widget, with a discount of 1 percent if paid within 30 days." The acceptance is the signed return of that agreement with any other agreed-to terms that come in along the way.

► Drafting a Contract

You may draft your own contract or have a professional draft it for you. If this is the case, you want to keep several points in mind. First, decide who will be the one to draw up the contract, and make sure everyone agrees whom that person will be. Next, start with a basic contract and work from there. You can either download one from the Internet or acquire one from a legal expert. Generic forms are free, such as living wills and demand for payment letters, but the more complex negotiating forms may come with hefty price tags. Some websites also allow you to view sample contracts like those used for business mergers.

▶ Note Taking

However you and the other party choose to have the contract drawn, you should always be thinking about what information you want to be clearly stated on the form. Taking notes from the beginning of the discussion right up until the signing of the contract prevents crucial details such as the following from being left out, muddled, misconstrued, or denied:

- Your and the other party's benefits—big and small
- Conditions on which these benefits are based
- Referenced material, such as price lists, warranty information, or insurance policies
- Important deadlines—both yours and the other party's
- Costs, prices, percentages, and other terms and conditions
- Terms for terminating and/or renegotiating the contract

The Power of Note Taking

A note about note taking: review your notes carefully, especially if someone else has rewritten them for you. There's always a chance one of your points was misinterpreted or left out.

Don't forget to jot down notes after each phone call, e-mail, and other communication. Also mark the date and time the initial contact took place so any changes that were discussed are on record. Make sure other parties to the negotiation allow sufficient time to capture key negotiation points results—especially in a split-second negotiation, it may be hard to get the time to record effectively.

In Charge of Writing

If you've been faithfully taking notes, you may or may not be chosen to put the final agreement together. This could be of great advantage to you, but it's a big role that may come with a lot of pressure.

▶ Benefits of Being the Contract Writer

In his book, *The Negotiation Toolkit: How to Get Exactly What You Want in Any Business or Personal Situation*, Roger J. Volkema suggests that offering to write up the agreement benefits you in two ways. First, it relieves the other party of the task and can be viewed as generous. Second, writing the agreement gives you some control over what it says and how it says it.

Run It by a Lawyer

Once you've written up the contract, have a lawyer look it over. The fees are probably minor and the expertise can be invaluable. Lawyers can spot mistakes, omissions, and uncertainties and can make the language more watertight where it makes sense.

▶ Third-Party Contract Writers

A third party can also be called in to write the contract. That third party can be a lawyer or business partner and should be impartial. It helps to have that person there through the negotiations to take his own notes and get a flavor for the deal.

Hammering Out the Details

Putting together a contract is almost as much fun as writing user manuals. The details are so minute that it's easy to zone out and overlook a few. There are some checkpoints you can put into place that will help you identify gaps as well as help you know what important information should be included.

Are Verbal Contracts Enforceable?

It's a critical question in today's split-second negotiating age. Many contracts can come about from a simple phone call or conversation on the golf course. State laws vary, but the baseline answer is "yes." If there is an offer, consideration, and acceptance, the contract is generally enforceable, with certain exceptions such as real estate contracts. Naturally, it helps to document the terms of the deal after the verbal agreement; otherwise enforcement is pretty difficult. If you do a lot of agreements on the fly, it's worth consulting an attorney to see whether your deals are in fact contracts. Also, it's important to realize that a commitment you make by phone or text or some other means may be enforceable, even if you don't intend it to be.

▶ Contingencies

The contract should spell out all details of agreed-to actions and compensation, as well as terms for termination or change, and in some cases, consequences for breach or violation of terms. In addition, you should ensure you and the other party know full well what the outcome will be if something unexpected happens. If there's a fire and the production facility is damaged before the job is done, how will you proceed? Will the contract become null and void?

▶ In Consideration

Consideration is a fancy term for tangible compensation or promises. As a standard principle of contract law, a contract is only legal and valid if something of value is exchanged for something else of value, and both parties must agree on all the terms. Even further, some states require that these considerations need to be in writing in order for the contract to be considered a legal document. "Consideration" includes any form of compensation—usually cash but it can be other tangible items. As a general principle, you must do something for the other party in order to require the other party to do something for you, or else it isn't really a contract.

What Does "Failure of Consideration" Mean?

Failure of consideration signifies the contract is breached. It means you or the other party didn't hold up your part of the bargain. For example, if you don't deliver a required deposit payment, the contract technically becomes null and void, and the person who has been wronged can withhold making good on her considerations and/or take legal action against the other party.

Reviewing the Contract

When the time comes for you to look over the contract, a careful review is important. It's a good idea to have an impartial colleague, and/or an attorney, go over it for details, commitments, and possible omissions. If something needs to be changed, have both parties initial all changes. Sign every page, and insist on an original copy if one isn't provided to you.

The Receipt Is the Contract

When you buy something at the store, your receipt is your contract. It states the time and date you made the purchases, what items were purchased, how much they cost (including tax), and the form of payment you used. Some receipts print the establishment's return policy on either the front or the back so you can't dispute their procedures.

▶ Dos and Don'ts

Following a few dos and don'ts helps you evaluate your contract and points out what should be double-checked. Use this list as a starting point to make sure you've covered your bases:

- Do crosscheck all documents and paperwork referred to in the contract.
- Do check for amendments the other party made—you'll need to initial these.

- Do make sure the other party has agreed to and signed your amendments—as much as you don't want any surprises, neither does anyone else.
- Do read the fine print.
- Do read all boilerplate material.
- Don't skip over sections because they look too exhausting to read.
- Don't forget to check the numbers—dates, prices, discounts, fees, and compensation.
- Don't assume that everything is correct.

Review and rework the contract as many times as you need to until you're completely satisfied. However, don't overwork it—you don't want to renegotiate everything if it's not necessary.

Meeting of Minds

When the final contract has been drawn and all amendments have been settled, there should be one final meeting with you, the other party, and the person who drafted the contract—either in person or using some virtual method.

Don't Be Rushed

Take your time, and don't feel pressured into signing the contract right away. On the other hand, if the other party is taking days to look over the contract and claiming the need to have his business partners, lawyers, family, and friends look it over, set a time limit after which the contract is void.

Contract Remedies

Assuming the deal was negotiated in good faith, and assuming that both parties are up to completing their end of the deal, and assuming there are no significant "mitigating circumstances" during the performance of the negotiated deal, the following discussion doesn't come into play. But negotiators and deal makers should be aware of what happens, or what *can* happen, if a negotiated contract goes awry. That knowledge, of course, helps you to make a better, more foolproof deal in the first place.

Contract law holds parties accountable for neglecting to satisfy their part of the deal. Let's say you and another person agree that in one week, you will buy his car for $5,000. You explain that you'll need to sell the car you currently own in order to get the $5,000. After the week is up and your car is sold, you go back to the car owner only to discover he's already sold the car to someone else for $6,000.

Though a written contract may not exist, a verbal promise was made in which you and the other party agreed to the details that were specified. You made plans based on that agreement, and contract law protects your right to perform acts that are contingent on those promises. It holds the other party responsible for failing to make good on his promise. Of course, if you have a written contract, your chances of proving your case are significantly greater.

▶ Withdrawing from the Contract

Most of us have experienced buyer's remorse at one point. You find something you like, buy it, then change your mind and decide you no longer want it. Usually, you can return the item to the store and get a refund, but it works differently with items that can't easily be returned, such as a house or a car.

When you enter into a business contract, a lot depends on what the other party is willing do. If you want to get out of the contract, the other party might simply allow it in order to maintain the integrity of the relationship. Maybe there was an oversight on your part, such as an accounting error that won't allow you to live up to your promises, or maybe something unexpected happened and your counterpart feels cutting you loose is the better choice. She also might have the foresight to know that if she doesn't let you out of the contract now, it may be difficult for you to live up to your side of the contract, thus making it more difficult for her to operate her business

Though your counterpart may be empathetic with your reasons for wanting to cancel the contract, she's not obliged to let you do it. If she decides not to let you out of the contract, you may need to hire a lawyer to discuss your options. If your counterpart wants to cancel the contract, use your judgment to decide if it's in your best interest to excuse her.

Cooling-Off Rule

The Federal Trade Commission (FTC) states that if you purchase an item of $25 or more outside of the retailer's permanent address and you change your mind about the transaction, you're entitled to a full refund within three days of the date of purchase. The rule applies to any sales that were made from your home, office, or dormitory, as well as hotel rooms and restaurants. There are many exceptions to this cooling-off rule, which can be reviewed at *www.ftc.gov* and should be if you engage in this kind of contract or negotiating, and it's a good example of the kind of legal principles and precedents that might enter into your negotiating and deal making—and a good reason to have lunch with an attorney from time to time.

Breach of Contract

A breach transpires when one party fails to perform what the contract states he has agreed to do. It occurs when the other party cannot perform her own duties; when the offending party does something that goes against what the contract states; or when the offending party simply will not do what's expected of her. You'll have to decide how severe the breach is before you decide to handle the matter in court.

For example, if your counterpart delivered goods three days past the agreed-upon ship date but the late shipment didn't harm your business, you might let it slide this time, discuss it with her to prevent it from happening again, and be on the lookout for any breaches that occur in the future. If, however, you decide that the breach is too significant to ignore, there are many options available to you.

▶ Specific Performance

In a court of law, the defendant may be ordered "specific performance"—to complete the terms of the contract rather than or in addition to paying damages. Note that this form of ruling is rarely made. It is reserved primarily for real estate cases in which the seller changes his mind and doesn't want to go through with the promise he made to the buyer. If it is granted, the offending party will have to deliver the goods, perform the job, and/or make the payment required of him in the contract.

▶ Resolution Options

There are many ways to get what was promised you, and most of them, not surprisingly, involve money. In addition to assessing the value of your losses, the judge might require the other party to pay any attorney fees that accrued from the time the contract was breached. He might also order the other party to pay "consequential and incidental damages," money awarded for losses that were predicted if a breach occurred. Going back to the car-sale example, since the car owner knew you were selling your old car in order to pay for the car he was selling you, and he sold the car to someone else anyway, he'll be required to pay these damages because he was aware of the contingency.

What Is a Tort?

A tort is similar to a breach of contract, but it usually concerns damages beyond the terms of the contract, as to reputation or physical ability of one of the parties to do something. It's a civil wrongdoing that requires a remedy from the court, usually beyond the terms of the contract.

Other remedies pertain to the state of the contract itself. If the judge decides on a "rescission" of the contract, the contract is canceled, all advancements are to be paid back, and all parties are no longer responsible for their portion of the terms.

Rules of Annulment

While you cannot be exonerated from poor business arrangements, judges will, in certain cases, annul an illegal contract. For example, if a sixteen-year-old signs a contract to buy a car, the contract is not binding because he is a minor and needs parental consent to sign it.

Good Faith or Bad Faith?

When two or more parties enter into a negotiation, it is under the assumption that all parties involved will be honorable and live up to their contractual commitments. Good faith also implies that everyone will be fair and truthful in order to satisfy the purpose of the initial meeting. When a party makes concessions she has no intention of fulfilling, she is acting in bad faith because she is deceptively giving the impression she is serious about the negotiation.

▶ Misrepresentation and Duress

If the other party tells you something he knows is false, and you sign the contract based on your belief that his statement is true, you can have the contract rescinded in court. The same holds true even if the other party was unaware that the information was false. Keep in mind that if you have the contract cancelled, you'll be required to give back any consideration you received. This includes money, products, keys to the company car, and warranties, to name a few.

A similar circumstance prevails if you signed a contract under duress. If you were drugged, held at gunpoint, or threatened in any way that made you sign against your will, the contract is not considered to be a legal document. A contract can only be valid if both parties willingly agree to its terms. It cannot be enforced if one party is made to do something he would not have done under ordinary conditions.

▶ Fraud

According to the *Merriam-Webster's Dictionary of Law*, the legal definition of fraud is "an intentional perversion of truth for the purpose of obtaining some valuable thing or promise from another." Similar to misrepresentation, fraud is an act in which a person presents false information, causing a counterpart to suffer one or many losses. The difference is that fraud is always intentional.

Fraud rears its ugly head in many situations, from social security claims to insurance policies. There are many laws and rules pertaining to this crime, including insider trading, which involves selling or purchasing securities (or stock) based on information that has not yet been made available to the general public. It's a criminal offense with severe punishment.

Dispute Resolution

Sometimes a misunderstanding simply won't go away, and the specter of litigation enters the picture. Filing a lawsuit shouldn't be a decision that's made in haste, and legal advice is important at this point. The litigation process differs by state and is beyond scope here.

Alternative Dispute Resolutions

Before resorting to litigation, contract law brings us alternative methods for resolving disputes outside of court, many of which involve some of the same negotiating skills that got you into the deal in the first place. Alternative dispute resolutions are, not surprisingly, geared towards resolving the dispute without the time, expense, and possible reputation damage of litigation. There are three methods available:

1. Negotiation and settlement

2. Mediation

3. Arbitration

Negotiation and settlement is a return to the negotiation table for the two parties originally involved. The second two methods involve a third party:

▶ **Mediation**

Mediation involves the intervention of a third party, called a mediator. While this can be someone who is highly knowledgeable in the issues being negotiated or mediated, the expertise often isn't necessary. Your mediator should be an expert in dispute resolution because her job is to help the disputing parties find some way to reach an agreement, especially when the negotiation is in deadlock.

The mediator offers a fresh perspective on the situation, which works towards a possible solution. Because she's working for both parties, she doesn't have a strong desire to hold on to certain concessions or make demands. Instead, the position she holds is to find the best possible "win-win" outcome based on the facts and objectives of the concerned parties.

Mediation is not a legal proceeding like a trial, and the mediator cannot decide on what the parties must agree to. It's a casual meeting in which the mediator talks to both parties together and then separately to help them refocus their attentions on their goals and tactics to reach them.

Mediators are brought into negotiations and disputes to avoid litigation, although if a lawsuit has already been filed, they might be brought in to avoid accruing more lawyer and court costs. Since all parties involved share the mediator's fees, it's often the most favorable and cost-effective choice.

Just like the contract that results from a negotiation, the mediated agreement is documented, signed, and enforceable by law. If the agreement is reached after a lawsuit has been filed, the court will receive a copy, and the case can be dismissed.

▶ Arbitration

Arbitration is similar to mediation in that it is a type of alternative dispute resolution that involves the inclusion of an outside party to help settle the dispute. In this case, however, the arbitrator directs a hearing and then decides who gets what. It's almost like litigation but is faster, cheaper, and more flexible. You don't have to worry about the court calendar and docket, and the parties can decide on the rules that will be in effect throughout the arbitration period.

For example, evidence that otherwise might not be allowed in court can be submitted in arbitration. Moreover, the parties can decide on who the arbitrators will be and whether the arbitration will be binding (parties must follow the arbitrator's final decisions) or nonbinding (parties take the award under advice and do not have to carry out the final decisions). Once the arbitration is finished, the resulting decision cannot be appealed. The conflict is considered resolved, and the case is closed.

Arbitrators

Anyone can be an arbitrator, as long as both parties agree. Typically, arbitrators are experts on the subject that is being discussed, trusted community members (such as spiritual leaders), or those who have many years of experience in law (such as retired judges or lawyers).

When choosing an arbitrator, look for a candidate with good written, oral, and organization skills as well as the ability to summarize information quickly and make intelligent decisions. It helps to review the track record of the arbitrator for experience congruent with your situation, as well as fast, friendly, and effective resolutions of similar disputes.

Split-Second Takeaways

1. Use notes from the negotiation to draft the contract.

2. Always try to be the person drafting the contract.

3. Always review the contract carefully, line by line.

Chapter 11
Negotiating for the Long Term

GOOD NEGOTIATING PRACTICE HAS the potential to create a win-win situation every time. That's why, whether you're buying a car or working out a vital business deal, it's important to avoid pitfalls and bad negotiating tactics. They can create bad will. Beyond the immediate benefit of emerging from a deal satisfied, there are long-term, indirect advantages to cultivating a win-win negotiating style.

Building Trust

Before you find yourself in your counterparts' good graces, you must first give them the opportunity to trust you. Once they feel you're trustworthy, you're in. Rapport develops more naturally because you've proven that you're not just "in it to win it," but you're in it to develop solutions that work. Once you've established that trust, it's important to maintain it.

Work to Build Trust

Some people will never trust you. It seems that no matter what lengths you go to, they simply do not budge. Maybe they had bad experiences with past negotiations and have trouble letting down their guard. Or maybe it's a front they use to avoid being taken at the negotiating table. Regardless of the reason, don't get discouraged. Continue to present yourself as someone to be trusted. Your counterpart will appreciate your professionalism.

The best way to gain your counterpart's trust is with actions that demonstrate your reliability and commitment. Just saying "You can trust me" or "I'm an honest person" won't sound very convincing. Worse, some may assume the opposite. You want the other party to pick up on your sincerity, and this can't happen if you come off too strong or too eager to make a good impression. It will be more difficult for you to work on the relationship if the other person is skeptical.

▶ Set the Tone

You want the other party to feel comfortable working with you right from the beginning. The first and most obvious way is to reinforce the win-win paradigm. Explain that you feel both of you have much more to gain by working together instead of against each other. If the other party agrees, be sure to show your enthusiasm. If you get resistance, ask for a discussion of the other party's main goal, and provide the reasons that your approach is the best way to reach it.

Check Your Watches

In a split-second negotiation, time is of the essence, not only for the negotiation itself but also for the negotiating parties. It's good to acknowledge that up front with your opponent, and set not only the ground rules but a general tone that fast is good; making a mutual pact not to waste each other's time.

How you present yourself can make all the difference when you enter the negotiation room. The way you carry yourself says a lot to your counterpart about the attitude you're taking toward the discussion and toward him. When you first see him, present a genuine smile, a firm handshake, and say something nice, like "How was your flight?" or "It's good to see you again." Such an approach can put the other party at ease while still maintaining an air of professionalism and trust.

Be Open

People will feel more relaxed if you are open and act friendly. It's also important to get the other person to open up; you can do this by asking encouraging questions—and listening to the answers. This will demonstrate that you're interested in what he has to say and that you are ready to listen to his concerns.

The atmosphere you create can influence your counterpart in deciding whether to trust you. If you break the ice by speaking first, you'll have the advantage of setting a positive tone. You can direct the conversation and get the agenda underway by asking questions related to specific topics.

▶ **Be Approachable**

No matter how much knowledge or leverage you have, throwing your weight around will only succeed in distancing your counterpart. Instead, relate to her by showing you are just as much a human being as she is. Express your feelings about any issue or possible outcome you don't agree with, but be sure to stay in control of your emotions, remaining calm and collected. Talk about why something doesn't work for you, and look for common elements that will help you come up with a solution that does. Portraying a positive attitude shows the other party that you're willing to look at problems from every angle in order to get to the bottom of them.

The more you open up, the more you show your counterparts your honest side, the more they'll trust you. Of course, you don't want to give everything away and make yourself a target, but you do want to let them know where you're coming from so they're aware of the challenges you have to face. You'll be able to work around the roadblocks and resolve differences more quickly.

If you want the other party to let his guard down a little, you'll have to do the same. Laughter is a great way to lighten up the mood in any situation, and it also gets people talking again. If you're stuck on an issue and you both feel you've exhausted every possible angle, find a way to joke about it. You'll begin to loosen up and hopefully be able to move on with the topic you're discussing.

That all said, don't spend too much time on the preliminaries. Remember, time is of the essence.

The Details Count

A small gesture can go a long way. You can establish a comfortable atmosphere by "setting the table" with a pitcher of cold water, dishes of candy, or other refreshments.

▶ **Say What You'll Do, Do What You Say**

When people say they'll get back to you, isn't it nice when they actually do? Dependable people are incredibly valuable. If your counterpart did not fulfill an obligation to the shipping company, you will have to delay the shipment of products to your customers, making them angry and possibly distrustful of your company's practices. Similarly, you'll begin to distrust your counterpart because of that failure to come through on an acknowledged duty.

No Empty Promises, Please!

Avoid making promises you aren't sure you can keep. If someone asks you a question that you can't answer, say that you'll look into the issue—and really mean it. Each time you make good on a promise, whether big or small, it will be remembered. The more you live up to your end of the deal, the more good things you say about your character.

A Collaborative Effort

Once you and the other party have established trust, you'll have an easier time working together without worrying about being manipulated. With each subsequent negotiation, this trust will grow deeper, and you'll be able to open up to each other even more. As a result, you'll be able to present more realistic ideas and create more effective solutions. Like any good relationship, it takes time to build a solid foundation. It also involves having to work through many struggles, helping each other every step of the way.

▶ Two Heads Are Better Than One

A good negotiator knows that the combined knowledge of all parties involved is more useful than that of only one party. This noncompetitive method of negotiating gives everyone the opportunity to voice their opinions, express their thoughts, and make a contribution to the final outcome. You're also more likely to understand each other's struggles and satisfy each other's needs, even if it means having to compromise when a win-win solution just isn't possible.

Pick-Up Tricks

What you learn from one negotiation could be applied to the next and might be used in a slightly different way. Suppose you're on an interview, and you pick up on the interviewer's strategy for avoiding the discussion of pay scale. You might find that it comes in handy on your next interview.

▶ Establishing the Possibilities

Brainstorming is a powerful collaborative tool, and helps when the goal is to discover an answer to solve both parties' problems. It's a process that allows you to look at old problems in new ways until you find something that works. The way to approach it is to get everything out in the open—ideas, examples, scenarios—and explore each option with more brainstorming. Your idea could spur your counterpart's idea, which will lead you to yet another idea, and so on. The result is a list of possibilities to examine further; the fact that this list of possibilities has been established jointly lends to the strength of this exercise, and sets the stage for more joint brainstorming sessions down the road.

While conventional brainstorming sessions are supposed to be open ended to foster the creation and retention of *all* ideas, in the split-second world it makes sense to set a time limit or an "idea limit," or else you might spend the entire day brainstorming!

Putting Ideas Into Practice

It's one thing for you and your counterpart to come to an agreement about how to decide on who gets what, but it's an entirely different thing to back up those words with actions. It's always possible that you're dealing with someone who only *appears* to want to play fair.

As concessions begin to be addressed, monitor the other party. Note the number of unfair tactics used or behaviors displayed that don't fall in step with win-win negotiating. If you must, clarify again what you're trying to do and how you both agreed to go about it. Once the other party realizes that you have your guard up, the negotiation will hopefully get back on track.

▶ Handling Conflicts

The success that comes from a good negotiation relies heavily on the success of finding the right interpersonal balance between you and the other party. You're bound to have conflicting points of view and opposing interests; handling them shrewdly is vital to your relationship. Win-win negotiating makes this possible. It is the best way to ensure the possibility of future dealings because it avoids creating a dichotomy at the negotiating table. For example, a mentality of strong/weak; better/worse; winner/loser does not exist because each party is considered equal and cooperates on the same level.

▶ Power of Example, Not Examples of Power

Power itself is not a negative thing to possess; rather, it's how people sometimes misuse power that gives it a bad reputation.

Using it to control other people is unethical and one-sided, while using it to produce a positive result is productive. Sometimes people have the power to make changes, but they don't use it because they're either unaware that they have it or they just don't make the effort. Using restraint, and exercising power through facts and accomplishments rather than harsh behavior and false pretense will go a long way towards better negotiations—and better relationships.

► **Stop, Look, and Listen**

Good listening habits are also critical to your negotiating relationships. Being a good listener not only shows other parties that you are sincere, it also encourages them to give you the same respect. Turn off your internal dialogue while your counterpart is speaking. Turn off your cell phone, or at least put it on vibrate and don't look at messages until after the discussion at hand.

Don't let your mind wander into how you're going to respond, what you plan to say about a point you want to make, or when you'll be able to pick up your kids. Really focus in on what you are being told, especially since the information you're getting might require some reading between the lines. Good listening skills not only aid the negotiation, but show the other parties that you're acting in good faith and are attentive to their needs, not just your own—a critical building block to a long-term relationship.

Enduring Relationships

Although short-term relationships should be treated respectfully, special attention should be paid to other parties with whom you'll need to or want to work with again in the future. When a contract ends, you may want to negotiate another, or you may want to modify an existing one.

Plan for the Long Run

A good rule of thumb is to always treat a negotiating or business relationship—even one generated in a simple phone call or e-mail dialogue—like it's a long-term relationship. You never know.

Once you've been working with someone for a while, you reach a point in which you both feel comfortable enough to make suggestions without worrying about how the other will react to them. It's important to hear each other out when suggesting a change or eliminating an idea altogether. Know that these suggestions are not meant to be offensive, so don't take them personally. When delivered from the appropriate person, this type of constructive criticism is merely another form of brainstorming. The other party is basically telling you which ideas work from that side of the table and which do not.

Your focus should always be on mutual satisfaction with every decision made. As with any other relationship, you must be willing to put your feelings out there and express the opinions and ideas you think work best.

Improving Your Skills

You should always come out of a negotiation feeling as if you've gained a little more knowledge and experience, both with the negotiating topic and with the negotiating parties involved. While there are many experts on the subject, no one is beyond learning something new and meeting someone new. The learning is enriched because people are different, circumstances are varied, and business practices and trends change constantly.

Fortunately, all these differences mean more experience under your belt. As for negotiating skills themselves, one way to increase your knowledge is to look at your past negotiations and pick out the things that worked for you and those that didn't—both in general and with the specific parties involved. This section covers several techniques for improving your negotiating skills and results.

Know Your Settlement Range

This should include all possible outcomes from your ideal to the worst-case scenario. Having this range helps you and your counterpart shift the discussion from negotiating to problem solving. If it's determined that the best possible outcome falls below your ideal but is still above your bottom line, consider it a win.

▶ Realistic Expectations

It's natural to have a lot of expectations, especially if you're not used to the process. You have your agenda set, your goals and objectives in order, your plan laid out, and your strategy in place. Then you get down to business, and you realize that some things are not what you predicted them to be. You might learn that the other party has an agenda of her own. She's being uncooperative and won't let you get a word in. This is when you learn how to adapt to the situation that's presented to you.

The negotiation process is not a science and does not follow a defined set of rules. Never assume that you know exactly what you're going to get from the other party. Having such expectations only prevents you from asking questions to learn more about her "real" position. Although it's safe to draw some general conclusions based on the information you've turned up in your research, it's risky to think you've got it all covered.

Your Report Card of Success

Using a grading system to measure your success is a good way to look back on the negotiation with a positive attitude and look forward to future negotiations with optimism. You don't want to beat yourself up over what you could've and should've done, but you do want to critique your performance by assessing the major points. How well did you prepare? How effective was your style? How quickly were you able to adapt to changes? Would you consider your relationship with the other party a good one?

Assess the Deal

Making an assessment allows you to step back and look at your overall presentation with a new perspective. Since the deal is done, you no longer feel the pressure to execute your strategy perfectly. Instead, you can step back and evaluate yourself objectively.

Remember not to be harsh on yourself. You want to feel good about the work you just did; otherwise, you'll only end up regretting your decisions and possibly not following through on your commitments. To conduct the evaluation without shaking your confidence in your abilities, look for things that need to be further developed. For example, make a note to work on your listening skills and remind yourself to ask more questions. Don't forget to celebrate the things that worked well for you. Your ability to make the other party feel comfortable with you is a huge victory.

Learn from Your Mistakes

Public speakers know that while they may beat themselves up for something they forgot to say or didn't say, the audience doesn't know what they didn't say! If you forget to bring up a point in a negotiation, but it doesn't materially affect the outcome, nobody else will ever know. If it did affect the outcome, well, lesson learned; perhaps you could have been better prepared or organized for the day of the show. Always try to look at yourself for what others saw, and for results, not for your performance per se.

▶ **Getting All A's**

The following list illustrates the most important points of negotiating, so give yourself an "A" for each one of the "A-skills" below you attained:

- Assembled the appropriate amount of information
- Achieved objectives and goals
- Acquired a greater knowledge and skill set with the topic(s) involved
- Advanced relationship with other negotiators
- Accomplished win-win solutions

Enjoying the Ride

You'll be surprised at how much enjoyment you derive from a good negotiation. Not only do you get the opportunity to achieve your goals, you get to work with (and learn from) some very talented and skilled people. Together, you and your counterpart embark on a journey of discovery and creativity in which the perfect plan is developed. Along the way, you engage in thought-provoking discussions that invigorate the mind and refresh the pool of ideas that you've amassed. As a result, the bonds you form help lead to agreements and further the possibility of future commitments.

Stay in Touch

Once the negotiation is complete, do you simply walk away and wait for the next contract or deal renewal? Most likely you shouldn't. In the interest of the long-term relationship, you should touch base every now and then to make sure everything is proceeding with your deal as it should. Not often enough to be annoying, but enough to ensure goodwill. Good big-ticket retail salespeople have figured this out. A phone call, e-mail, or text every few months or so can do a lot to preserve and build the relationship—and to make things easier the next time around.

As a brief summary, to not only succeed at a negotiation but also to preserve and build a long-term relationship, especially in today's socially connected, fast-paced environment:

- Think win-win
- Think "golden rule"—do unto others as you would have them do unto you
- Prepare well
- Listen and communicate well
- Be collaborative
- Be honest
- Make good use of time—yours and theirs
- Be professional throughout

Split-Second Takeaways

1. Work to build trust with your negotiating partners.

2. Stick to your commitments; do what you say you'll do.

3. Constantly strive to improve your negotiating skills.

Appendix
Sample Negotiation Scripts

During negotiations, it's always important to listen and respond to the requests of the person you are negotiating with. However, it never hurts to have a few key phrases in your back pocket so you have someplace to start when you're caught off guard. The following sample scripts will give you such key terms and phrases that you may find helpful in your future negotiations.

Sample Script—
Dealing with Difficult People

Imagine a negotiating session that goes something like this.

Ms. Salesperson: Good afternoon. I'm glad you could make the time to see me. I'm sure you won't regret it.

Mr. Grouchy: Well, I'm not so sure. Frankly, I've got a very busy afternoon and I don't have much time to waste. I'm really not sure there's any point in our speaking. Sorry to speak bluntly, but that's the way I am.

Ms. Salesperson: I certainly understand that your schedule is very compressed. I'll be brief as I can. We've dealt with your company before, and I understand that you've agreed to take delivery of 10,000 units. As I see it what we really need to settle here is the issue of delivery date and warranty.

Mr. Grouchy: Not so fast, not so fast. Who told you we were going to take 10,000 units?

Ms. Salesperson: That's the figure that was given in the deal memo that . . .

Mr. Grouchy: Well, I can tell you right now that we're taking only 5,000 units, and only if you can guarantee delivery by next week. If you can't do a deal along those lines, we might as well stop talking right now.

Ms. Salesperson: I . . .

Mr. Grouchy: There's no point in arguing about it. That's my position, and I'm sticking to it. The only question is if you can meet these terms or not.

Ms. Salesperson: (pausing for a moment) Sir, I'm sorry if there's been a misunderstanding between our two companies. Believe me, I want to do what's best for you as well as for my company. But I think we should recognize that we're really in this together. We have a common goal, and we need to work toward it.

Mr. Grouchy: What common goal is that?

Ms. Salesperson: Well, you need these units delivered in a timely fashion, and my company can supply them. We just need to arrive at a solution that works for both of us. I think if we're flexible and focus on our mutual benefit we can work something out.

Mr. Grouchy: All right. What are you suggesting?

Ms. Salesperson: Your representative had indicated previously that you were willing to take delivery of 10,000 units, but since you're saying now you only need 5,000 units, I'm assuming something has changed. Can you tell me what about your needs is different?

Mr. Grouchy: Things have changed since we talked to you people before. We're no longer servicing five out of the twenty stores that are on our list. Those five stores are closing this month, so our needs are less.

Ms. Salesperson: That makes a difference, of course. But you'll need some backup inventory all the same, won't you?

Mr. Grouchy: We can just order that from you when we need it.

Ms. Salesperson: But it will be more expensive to make a series of smaller orders, won't it? Even with the increased warehousing costs of storing surplus inventory? Though I can understand the need to find the right balance between an appropriate inventory and running into shortages that could cause delays in supplying your retailers. Why don't we meet in the middle and say 7,500 units?

Mr. Grouchy: Okay, that would probably work, but what about delivery? This whole thing has dragged on too long, and if we can't get delivery by next week I don't think that there's a point in doing a deal for any units because we won't be able to move them into the stores in time.

Ms. Salesperson: When next week is the latest you could take delivery?

Mr. Grouchy: We could move them through the warehouse processing system in a day and a half. If they're going to be in the stores for the weekend and we allow one day for delivery, that means we'd need them in the warehouse by Wednesday noon at the absolute latest.

Ms. Salesperson: I'll have to speak to my supervisors to make sure that's possible, but we might be able to manage that. I know it's important to accommodate your delivery schedule. If that tight of a turnaround proves difficult for us, are there some other options we could examine?

Mr. Grouchy: Well, could we ship directly from your warehouse to the stores? That would save us a day and a half.

Ms. Salesperson: That's an interesting idea. It might raise some process issues, since we don't have the stores programmed into our system, but I can certainly look into that. If we elect to go that route, would you be willing to pay a somewhat higher per unit cost?

Mr. Grouchy: How much are you thinking?

Ms. Salesperson: What about ten cents per unit?

Mr. Grouchy: We could do five cents.

Ms. Salesperson: Let me run some numbers. I think we could get that down to seven cents per unit with a discount on shipments to individual stores that were 1,000 units or above.

Mr. Grouchy: Yes, that would work.

Ms. Salesperson: Great. Regarding the warranty, if we go with the second scenario we'd start the warranty as soon as the products reached the stores rather than when they entered your warehouse, since we'd be bypassing that. Is that okay with you?

Mr. Grouchy: Yes, I guess that would be okay.

Ms. Salesperson: Wonderful. Mr. Grouchy, I appreciate your time and willingness to work things out to our mutual benefit.

Mr. Grouchy: Oh, that's fine. Sorry I was a bit harsh with you when we started. There's been a lot of stress around here this week.

Ms. Salesperson: Not at all. I'm glad we could arrive at a tentative agreement. I'll confirm these points with my boss and give you a call tomorrow morning. Does 10 A.M. work for you?

Mr. Grouchy: Yes, that'll be fine.

Note the following points about this negotiating session:

1. The salesperson didn't let Mr. Grouchy intimidate her; instead, she used calming, neutral phrases to defuse the situation and turn the discussion to the specifics of the negotiation.

2. The salesperson asked for specifics of the situation, operating from facts rather than emotions and stressing the need to find a mutually satisfactory solution.

3. Neither side in the negotiation gave anything away for free. Any concessions were matched by a request for a concession from the other side.

4. The salesperson made clear she would have to get agreement from her boss to the new terms, and she set a specific time for a follow-up conversation with the customer.

Both sides were willing to meet in the middle to find a win-win solution; neither side showed any interest in positional negotiating, which would have created a stalemate.

Sample Script—
Tricks, Traps, and Tactics

Let's say you're discussing doing a deal with a new vendor. You're dealing with two salespeople: Mr. Bark and Mr. Bright. The conversation might go something like this:

Mr. Smallbiz: Thanks for taking the time to discuss this with me. We're very interested in the services your company has to offer, and I hope we can come to an arrangement.

Mr. Bark: Let's get going with this. We don't have much time. We've got two more meetings this afternoon with other companies.

Mr. Smallbiz: Certainly. Now, as you know we're looking for a supplier who can provide us with 5,000 widgets a month, increasing to 8,000 widgets a month in April when our other four stores are up and running. In other words, for the year we're looking at . . .

Mr. Bark: Eighty-four thousand units for the year. Yes, I know that. I can count. Let's get on with it.

Mr. Bright: Well, let's not get too impatient, Mr. Bark. I'm sure Mr. Smallbiz has prepared very thoroughly for this meeting.

Mr. Bark: Just get on with it, okay. I've got a lot to do. Eighty-four thousand units is possible, but we'd have to put on an additional shift when you increase your demand. So the smallest number we can meet is fifteen cents per widget.

Mr. Smallbiz: What? But the number I was quoted . . .

Mr. Bark: That's the number we can do. Take it or leave it.

Mr. Bright: Mr. Bark, why don't you go take care of your other meeting and I'll keep things going here.

Mr. Bark: Okay. But remember what I said: Fifteen cents a unit. That's the bottom line. (Leaves)

Mr. Bright: Mr. Smallbiz, I'd like to apologize for Mr. Bark's attitude. He's under a lot of pressure just now, and I'm sure he didn't mean to sound like that.

Mr. Smallbiz: I can excuse being under pressure, but there was no call at all to behave that way. Frankly, if this is the way he's going to behave, I'm not sure I can do business with you.

Mr. Bright: Well, I'm sure you and I can work something out. Now what unit price did you have in mind?

Mr. Smallbiz: What I was thinking was . . .

Mr. Bright: I'm sorry to interrupt, but I did want to say that I think Mr. Bark's number of fifteen cents per unit is a bit high. I know he wants to hold the line on that, but between you and me I think we could come down a bit, since we're very anxious to have your business.

Mr. Smallbiz: What number were you thinking you could get to?

Mr. Bright: Well, I can't promise anything until I talk to Mr. Bark—and you saw what *he's* like—but I think we could probably go down to eleven cents a unit. It might take a bit of arguing on my part, but I think I could get him to go that low if I catch him at the right time.

Mr. Smallbiz: Well, that sounds pretty reasonable. But let me tell you what my concerns are. My CFO is pretty rigid when it comes to the numbers. And he's said that we'd really need these widgets to come in at eight cents a unit.

Mr. Bright: That's a very low price. I don't know if we could sustain that.

Mr. Smallbiz: I see. Well, I understand. Thanks a lot for your time.

Mr. Bright: Wait just a minute. Let me punch up some numbers here. I think with a little bit of creativity on our part, we could get to nine cents a unit. Would that work for you?

Mr. Smallbiz: I think so. The CFO might put up a bit of a fight, but I can tell him that you went to the mat for me here, so I think he'd go along.

Mr. Bright: I'd certainly appreciate that. Now, could we discuss delivery dates?

Mr. Smallbiz: Sure. It takes approximately ten days for units to be processed through our warehouse and shipped to our outlets. So we'd need to take delivery of the first shipment of widgets on December 1 so they can be in stores by December 11.

Mr. Bright: Normally that would be fine, but because that's in the middle of the holidays we're going to have to charge a shipping premium of $2,000.

Mr. Smallbiz: That's significantly higher than our other vendors. Could we get that down a bit?

Mr. Bright: We can't lower it, but I can certainly throw in something extra—for instance, we could extend the warranty on the first shipment of units an extra week.

Mr. Smallbiz: That's generous, but I understand that your company pretty much always extends the warranty for first-time shipments; that's what you've done for your other customers. So it sounds as if you wouldn't be really giving us anything special.

Mr. Bright: What did you have in mind instead?

Mr. Smallbiz: How about an extended warranty on the first three months' shipments?

Mr. Bright: Let's say the first two months. Then I think we've got something.

Mr. Bark: (re-entering) Okay, let's get back to business. Mr. Smallbiz, I've been talking to some of my people. And the units you want will have to be tied to a shipment of our widgetwinders.

Mr. Smallbiz: What do you mean?

Mr. Bark: I mean that if you want to take consignment of the widgets, you'll also have to accept a consignment of widgetwinders with them.

Mr. Smallbiz: This is the first I've heard of this.

Mr. Bark: Look, I'm tired of talking about this. If you take the widgets, you take the winders. Okay? Yes or no.

Mr. Smallbiz: (after a pause) Mr. Bark and Mr. Bright, I think the best thing here would be to take a break. Let's stop for ten minutes while I make some phone calls to my people and then we can start over again. In light of this new information, we'll have to see on what terms we can still do a deal.

Some things to notice:

1. Mr. Bark and Mr. Bright are playing a classic good-cop/bad-cop routine with Mr. Smallbiz. It's very possible that they've worked all this out before Mr. Smallbiz even walked into the room.

2. Mr. Smallbiz, cleverly, doesn't fall for it. Instead, he counters with two tactics: first, he creates his own bad cop (the ominous CFO); second, he threatens to break off negotiations, which quickly brings Mr. Bright back to the table.

3. Each party makes concessions, but Mr. Bright tries to make a false concession—something he would have given away anyway—in the form of the extended warranty agreement. Mr. Smallbiz calls him on it and gets things back on track.

4. Mr. Bark tries to put Mr. Smallbiz off his stride by interrupting the negotiations and throwing in a new twist: the add-on of the widgetwinders. Mr. Smallbiz, sensibly, doesn't react. Instead he asks for some time out for everyone to cool down. Once they reconvene, he'll be in a better position to negotiate from the head rather than from the gut.

Sample Script—
Be Prepared

Let's consider the dangers of entering a negotiation unprepared and without a clear sense of what you want and how to get it. Meet Mrs. Eatwell, who owns a small chain of restaurants. Recently she's been approached by the owners of a much larger restaurant chain about merging the two businesses. As the curtain rises, Mrs. Eatwell, who's been too busy to properly prepare for this negotiation, is meeting with Ms. Executive, representing the Big Kahuna restaurant company.

Ms. Executive: Good morning, Mrs. Eatwell. Nice to see you. Well, let's get down to business, shall we?

Mrs. Eatwell: Uh, sure.

Ms. Executive: Now, we've already gone over in our previous meeting the advantages to both of us of a merger between our two organizations. I suggest in this meeting we drill down a bit and talk about some specifics. We can discuss personnel, vendors, and timing. I think that should pretty well fill up our time, don't you?

Mrs. Eatwell: Sure, I guess so. Do you think we should also talk about publicity and how we're going to announce this?

Ms. Executive: No, we can save that until our next session. So. Personnel. Now what is your current headcount?

Mrs. Eatwell: To tell you the truth, I'm not quite sure. We've got five stores, and I think they each have a staff of about, uh . . .

Ms. Executive: According to my research, your total headcount is 132. Does that sound right?

Mrs. Eatwell: Yes, I think so. I'd have to verify that, but that sounds like it might be the case.

Ms. Executive: Now I'm also showing that your restaurants have staffs, respectively, of twenty-two, nineteen, twenty-six, eighteen, and twenty-nine. Is that right?

Mrs. Eatwell: Yeah, probably.

Ms. Executive: That's a total of, let me see, 114 people actually working in the restaurant. So that means that you have a corporate staff of eighteen people.

Mrs. Eatwell: Uh huh.

Ms. Executive: That's a very large staff for a relatively small organization. And once the merger goes through, some of the positions will be duplicated. So I think we need to see which of your people would be let go immediately once we announce the merger.

Mrs. Eatwell: Now, wait a minute. Why would it have to be all my people who are let go? Let's consider whether some of my staff might have more experience than your people.

Ms. Executive: Well, I have to keep in mind that we have made strong commitments to our people that this merger will benefit them. I don't see how we can turn around and tell them that the benefit is they've lost their job.

Mrs. Eatwell: Well, I've made commitments to my people too. I don't want to see people lose jobs they've worked very hard at.

Ms. Executive: Look, I don't want us to get into a stalemate over this.

Mrs. Eatwell: Neither do I. What about this: We consider which positions are duplicated and make a decision in each case based on the experience and skill set of the people involved. Then, before letting the other individual go, we try to find another place they can fit in to the organization. We give them priority over any possible new hires, and if there's just no way to keep them on board, then we let them go.

Ms. Executive: Yes, I think that would work. I suggest that the decisions about this be made by a joint committee of our two organizations. My head of HR can contact your people and set this up once we're ready to go ahead with the merger.

Mrs. Eatwell: That sounds okay.

Ms. Executive: What we'd ideally like to see for the merged organization is a staff of no more than thirty. We feel this could best serve the needs of the new company and would keep us sufficiently lean so that we'd have some room for expansion in the future if business warrants it. Is that acceptable?

Mrs. Eatwell: I think so.

Ms. Executive: Now, as regards vendors. Your main food supplier at present is Gigafood, is that right?

Mrs. Eatwell: Yes. We've worked with them for a number of years.

Ms. Executive: Our supplier has been Supercaloric, and we have an exclusive agreement with them that extends until June two years from now. So . . .

Mrs. Eatwell: Excuse me. I think we need to look at this a different way. You were going to propose that we drop Gigafood in favor of Supercaloric, is that right?

Ms. Executive: Yes.

Mrs. Eatwell: But that breaks a long relationship that my company has had with a vendor. And I think that you'd agree that ending these sorts of relationships abruptly could cause a lot of bad feelings that's not in anyone's interests. Right?

Ms. Executive: I see your point, but I think . . .

Mrs. Eatwell: Sorry, just let me continue here a moment. Rather that make this an either/or proposition, I think it would be better if we could find a way to work this out so we both get something out of the new arrangement. I don't want to drop Gigafood, though I understand your need to maintain your contract with Supercaloric. But in the terms of that contract, there must be some provision for revisiting the contract if the structure of your organization changes. Is that the case?

Ms. Executive: Yes, I believe that's the case. I'd have to review the exact terms of the contract to be sure.

Mrs. Eatwell: So let me suggest this: For the next two years, the length of your contract with Supercaloric, they will continue to supply your restaurants. However, we'll drop certain items that they supply and instead give those to Gigafood. Essentially, both vendors will be supplying the merged chain. At the end of the two years, we can review the experience and discuss whether or not to negotiate an exclusive contract with one vendor or the other. That way we both win, and the vendors win too, because they're continuing to keep their business.

Ms. Executive: I'll have to take this back to my board, but I think that's a very workable solution, Mrs. Eatwell.

Poor Mrs. Eatwell. In the first part of the discussion, Ms. Executive ran all over her. A few things to note about this conversation:

1. In the first exchange between the two parties, we see the result of poor preparation; Mrs. Eatwell doesn't have the facts and figures at her fingertips, as does Ms. Executive. The result is that she comes off stronger and gets what she wants.

2. Ms. Executive takes control of the meeting from the beginning, effectively setting the agenda and thus gaining the upper hand in the negotiation.

3. Initially Mrs. Eatwell's responses tend to be in the form of questions or tentative responses. It's not until the second half of the conversation that she asserts himself. When she does, the negotiation swings back in her direction, and she's able to win some points.

4. Mrs. Eatwell finds a way out of the stalemate by proposing a solution in which both parties gain something.

Sample Script—
Closing with Confidence

Even at the end of a deal, things can go wrong. But, as we'll see here, there are ways to make sure your closing stays on track and you finish with an agreement that works for both of you. Let's listen in on two executives negotiating a new partnership agreement between their firms.

Ms. Bigshot: Okay, I think we've got these numbers wrapped up. We're in agreement on the basic points here, right?

Mr. Indecisive: Well, I think so, but I'm still a bit concerned about how the weekly exchange of sales numbers is going to work. Because we don't update our numbers until Friday, but you said you needed the information on Thursday.

Ms. Bigshot: Right. We went over that, if you remember. We can push our reporting deadline back a day to accommodate your schedule.

Mr. Indecisive: Oh, yes, that's right.

Ms. Bigshot: So I think we can move to close this up at this point. Let me just reiterate the main points of agreement: We'll begin this partnership on March 6, and it will run for eighteen months. At the end of that time, we'll reevaluate and determine whether we want to continue or not. During the eighteen months, your customers will receive our widgets at a 20-percent discount, and our customers will be able to purchase widgetwinders at a 15-percent discount, with an extra 5-percent discount on orders of 500 or more. We'll announce this agreement in a press release this Saturday. . . .

Mr. Indecisive: Wait, wait. Did we agree to that timing?

Ms. Bigshot: Yes. We talked about this before, that we want to get the word out quickly so our customers can begin to make their purchase plans before the summer selling season hits.

Mr. Indecisive: Yes, I remember we talked about that. But I'm still nervous about it. I mean, I've got to get this past our board, and I wonder if they're going to be very quick to approve it.

Ms. Bigshot: I see your point. Is there anything I can do to help? For instance, I could pull together some of the figures I presented to you at our last meeting and put them in a PowerPoint presentation that you could show to the board. I'd also be happy to draw up a memorandum from our board summarizing the advantages of this arrangement in terms of increased revenue for both companies.

Mr. Indecisive: Yes, that would be helpful. I'd appreciate it.

Ms. Bigshot: Great! Consider it done.

Mr. Indecisive: But do you think we should wait another couple of weeks before finalizing everything? Just to give this deal time to settle and let everyone think about it some more.

Ms. Bigshot: We could do that, but I think we'd be throwing away an opportunity. The truth of the matter is that deals like this depend heavily on timing, and if we don't move now it raises questions about whether it's worth setting up this partnership at all.

Mr. Indecisive: Yes, I see your point. And I assure you, we really do want to do this.

Ms. Bigshot: Here's my suggestion. I'll draw up a deal memorandum that embodies all the points we've agreed on. I'll send it to you by end of business day tomorrow. I'll also include the material I mentioned earlier, the facts and figures in a PowerPoint that you can submit to your board. While you're looking that over, I'll have my people start drawing up the contract. They can send over the draft to you by the day after tomorrow, and you'll have that to look at while your board is considering the issue.

Mr. Indecisive: Yes . . . yes, I think that would probably work.

Ms. Bigshot: The other thing I think we can get to work on right away is the press release. I'll have my PR people draft it and then send it on to you. That way, everything will be in place and ready to roll out Saturday when your board approves this partnership.

Mr. Indecisive: *If* they approve it, you mean.

Ms. Bigshot: No, I mean **when**. I have a lot of confidence they'll go for what we've agreed on here. I think we've done a very good, thorough job of hashing out the various issues and reviewing the numbers. I have to tell you, Mr. Indecisive, that I believe in this partnership. It's going to result in substantial sales for both our companies, and it will expand our geographic reach so that we both benefit from tapping a new customer pool.

Mr. Indecisive: You may very well be right. I know that sometimes it's hard to see the forest for the trees, and I can certainly see the benefits of this arrangement. I just don't want to get rushed into anything I'll regret later.

Ms. Bigshot: Mr. Indecisive, here's the bottom line: I've been in this business a long time, and I know you have too. We both know that trying to make bad deals doesn't benefit anyone in the end. If I didn't believe—really believe—that this deal was the right thing for both of us, I wouldn't do it. Because if it's a bad deal for you and we go through with it, I'll be destroying my relationship with your company, and that's not going to do me any good in the long run. At the end of the day, all I've got is my integrity, and I'm standing on that when I tell you that we should create this partnership. Not just because it's good for my company, but because it's good for *both* companies.

Mr. Indecisive: I believe you, Ms. Bigshot. I think we have a deal. Let's put it to bed.

At the end of a prolonged negotiation, there's nothing more annoying than someone who wants to start all over again. Fortunately, in this case, Ms. Bigshot is able to cut off Mr. Indecisive at the pass and corral him back into inking the deal. Some things to note:

1. Ms. Bigshot never loses her temper, although it must be tempting. Instead, she approaches the problem of Mr. Indecisive's wavering as a matter of finding out how to help the other party come to an agreement.

2. By being decisive and having plenty of suggestions, Ms. Bigshot is able to keep the tone of the discussion positive and moving forward. If she'd reacted with anger or negativity to

Mr. Indecisive, it's quite possible the deal could have blown up in these closing moments. Instead, it goes ahead.

3. Ms. Bigshot suggests that her company draw up the initial drafts of all the paperwork, in this way controlling the terms of the deal.

4. A jolt of enthusiasm and a reminder of the importance of honesty in business dealings finish the meeting on a high note.

Sample Script—
The Devil's in the Details

There are a lot of advantages to being the one to draft the contract. Even though the contract is still subject to negotiation, you've had the first chance to frame the terms of the discussion.

Let's listen in on an initial discussion of a contract between an editor and an author, trying to work out terms for publishing a book.

Mr. Editor: I sent you a copy of our contract last week, and I'm hoping you've had a chance to look at it and see that it reflected our discussions about your project.

Ms. Bestseller: Yes, I did, thanks. I've got some questions, if you don't mind.

Mr. Editor: Fire away.

Ms. Bestseller: First of all, could I ask where the language for this came from? It seems awfully, well . . . legal.

Mr. Editor: That's because it is. This is based on our standard boilerplate contract that we use with all authors. We just adapt the language and terms to the person we're negotiating with, but the basic language has been prepared by our legal team. I know it seems kind of roundabout and legalese-y, but the lawyers are concerned to protect everyone's interests. Including yours, by the way.

Ms. Bestseller: Well, I appreciate that, but just to be on the safe side I ran this by my lawyer as well, and that's where some of these questions are coming from.

Mr. Editor: Okay.

Ms. Bestseller: For instance, let's look up here in the first paragraph where it says that the Author (me) agrees to deliver a manuscript of no less than 55,000 words.

Mr. Editor: Right.

Ms. Bestseller: Didn't we agree that the manuscript would only be 45,000 words? It seems concerning to me to suddenly add 10,000 words onto a contract. After all, that's quite a lot of writing, given that the deadline is very tight.

Mr. Editor: Let me check my notes. Hmmm. It looks as if you're right. We agreed to 45,000 words. However, I'd like to keep this a little flexible. Could we say a range of 45,000 to 50,000 words?

Ms. Bestseller: I think so, but that raises another point. Here in the fourth paragraph . . .

Mr. Editor: I'm sorry to interrupt, but while we're thinking about it could you cross out 45,000 words and substitute "between 45,000 and 50,000 words" and then put your initials next to that? That'll make everything legal in the final signed document.

Ms. Bestseller: Sure. No problem. I'll make that change on all the copies of the contract before I send them back to you. But now down here in paragraph four it says that if I don't deliver by the deadline of May 1, I'll be penalized by having to forego 25 percent of the advance on the book. Considering I just agreed to possibly deliver an additional 5,000 words of text, it seems to me that it's not quite right to hold me to this deadline at the possible cost of part of the advance.

Mr. Editor: I see your point, but at the same time I have to ensure that you'll deliver the manuscript in a time frame that works for our production schedule on this book.

Ms. Bestseller: Could we push that deadline back a week to May 8? I'd be confident in delivering a completed manuscript by then, and if I don't, I'm willing to be penalized.

Mr. Editor: Yes, that would be okay. Please make that change and initial the contracts.

Ms. Bestseller: Okay. Now in this section on page five it says that royalties are based on net proceeds from sales. I don't quite understand what that means. I wonder if you could explain it to me a bit.

Mr. Editor: Sure. Bookstores buy from us on consignment, and if, after a couple of months, they need to lower their inventory for a particular book, they return the excess books to us. That's what the term "returns" refers to. Our royalty payments to you are based, as much as we can figure, on the total net sales to the bookstores—that is, our initial sell-in minus returns. Does that make sense?

Ms. Bestseller: Yes, I see now. Okay, I just wanted some clarification on that point. After all, I don't want to put my name on something I don't understand.

Mr. Editor: Absolutely. If there's anything unclear in the contract, we should get it out of the way right now.

Ms. Bestseller: So along the same lines, could you just explain what happens if I deliver the manuscript to you and you don't like it?

Mr. Editor: Well, just to be clear: If you don't deliver the book to us at all, that would be a breach of contract and we'd have the right to withhold your advance, since you broke the terms of the agreement. If you send us the manuscript and we review it and decide it's not publishable, then we'll give you some time to fix it, as specified in the contract under paragraph three. You can see that it's all spelled out there. If, after you've had time to fix it, it's still not ready to be published, then we consider you in breach of contract, since you were supposed to provide something we could publish and you didn't. If you fix it, of course, all is well and good, and we just proceed as if nothing happened.

Ms. Bestseller: I see. That makes sense. As long as I have a reasonable amount of time to fix it, of course. I see here that I have thirty days. Isn't that awfully short?

Mr. Editor: That's pretty standard in the industry. It's what we always use, because if we put things off and give you a lot more time, that can create a lot of scheduling problems for us, and ultimately that won't be good for the book's sales.

Ms. Bestseller: Well, I guess I'll just have to turn in a perfect first draft then. I think that's all the questions I had. I'll sign these and send them along to you tomorrow.

As you can see from this discussion, even at the contract stage, negotiations are continuing. You can also see that:

1. Ms. Bestseller did the right thing in asking questions about anything in the contract that was unclear. Legal language

can often be convoluted, and if you don't ask what something means, you might be disappointed to find out the answer when it's too late.

2. Both Mr. Editor and Ms. Bestseller exhibited flexibility in their responses. The contract stage is no time to start practicing positional negotiating.

3. The contract clearly spells out the consequences of a breach of contract. This is essential, since both parties have to know from the start what it will mean if one or the other doesn't live up to his or her end of the bargain.

Sample Script—
Negotiate with Confidence

Ms. Salesexec is working out a deal with Mr. Superstore regarding the delivery of product during the Christmas holidays. Watch the back-and-forth flow of the discussion between them to see how they overcome obstacles.

Ms. Salesexec: So what we have to decide is the schedule on which we can make September deliveries, right?

Mr. Superstore: Yes. This is going to be tricky, because we've got a lot of sales going on over the Christmas holidays, and we need to have all the merchandise in the warehouse by the beginning of October.

Ms. Salesexec: But then you're increasing your warehousing costs by having to store the product for three months. Couldn't you take delivery a month later? That would ease things for us on the production end.

Mr. Superstore: Well . . .

Ms. Salesexec: Please let me know if this doesn't work for you. I think it's important that we be completely honest here. If an arrangement doesn't work, it's not going to benefit either one of us.

Mr. Superstore: The thing is that we've scheduled to take on extra staff at the warehouse in October. We estimate that with our new computer systems and fulfillment systems, it'll take us a month or so to get everything fully up and running, and we want your product in the warehouse to make sure our people know how to handle it. We've got to give them a little time to find their feet.

Ms. Salesexec: I understand where you're coming from. What concerns me is that to meet the earlier deadline we'd have to add staff to our production facilities, and that would push the price per unit up.

Mr. Superstore: To what?

Ms. Salesexec: I'll have to double-check with our people, of course, but I think we could be looking at a per-unit increase of ten to fifteen cents.

Mr. Superstore: That's quite a bit. Are you sure it would be that much?

Ms. Salesexec: Not entirely. As I say, I'll have to go back and crunch some numbers with the production folks. But the fact is that what you're proposing is a very early date for us, and I just don't know if we can make it.

Mr. Superstore: What kind of flexibility do you have on that?

Ms. Salesexec: I really don't have any, to be honest. These numbers are going to be what they are, and I'm afraid you'll just have to take my word on this. However, let's see if we can find another solution to the problem. Do you need the full order delivery in September?

Mr. Superstore: We could probably look at a partial delivery. How much did you have in mind?

Ms. Salesexec: Well, assuming that we keep our staff at its current levels, I'd say we could fulfill approximately 50 percent of the order by the beginning of September. That would give your staff something to work with, and by the time they went through that amount of product, we could deliver another 25 percent of the order by the first of October and the final 25 percent by mid-October.

Mr. Superstore: That would probably work, but it might create some pacing problems for us. Would you be supplying all the parts that we'd need to ship or would the order come in with just one kind of part followed by another?

Ms. Salesexec: What would work better for you?

Mr. Superstore: Obviously we'd prefer to be able to start shipping to our outlets as soon as possible, given our schedule, so I'd rather have a partial order from you that contains everything we need to begin that shipping process.

Ms. Salesexec: I think that can happen, but this will mean re-tooling some of our production process, so again you're going to be looking at a price increase.

Mr. Superstore: How much for this one?

Ms. Salesexec: With the caveats I told you before—I've got to crunch these numbers and run them by Production and Finance—I think we could probably do this for a per-unit cost of five cents.

Mr. Superstore: Well, that's a lot better than ten to fifteen cents.

Ms. Salesexec: Much better. Do you think this arrangement could work?

Mr. Superstore: I think so. It sounds as if what we need is a clear, firm delivery schedule and a chance to prepare everyone on our teams to meet it. I'd like to see the contract include as an appendix a guaranteed schedule with specifications as to penalties for not meeting it, since I have to be able to assure everyone on my team that we're protected financially if something goes wrong on the production end.

Ms. Salesexec: I don't see that as a problem. When I have our legal people draft the contract, I'll have them put together that schedule, and you and I can go over the details when we review the contract.

Mr. Superstore: Great! Ms. Salesexec, good doing business with you.

Ms. Salesexec: And with you, Mr. Superstore.

As this chapter has pointed out, negotiations work best when both sides are honest with each other and specify precisely what they want and why they need it. In this instance:

1. Mr. Superstore explained the problem on his end to Ms. Salesexec and told her what his overall goal was. The result was that she was able to propose a solution that worked for him.

2. Each party in the discussion was respectful of the other's viewpoint and didn't interrupt or badger—both of these are no-nos in negotiation, though as explained in an earlier chapter you may encounter these as tactics employed by an intimidator.

3. Both sides were willing to give in order to get—the essence of win-win negotiation techniques. As a result, Mr. Superstore

and Ms. Salesexec will both probably have good holiday seasons, and their two companies will continue to maintain a productive working relationship with one another.

Index